hey FRIEND

31 JOURNALING DEVOTIONS ON FRIENDSHIP

B&H
PUBLISHING GROUP
Brentwood, Tennessee

Is any pleasure on Earth
as great as a circle of
Christian friends?

—C. S. Lewis

I would rather walk
with a friend in the
dark than walk alone
in the light.

—Helen Keller

Two are better than one because
they have a good reward for their
efforts. For if either falls, his
companion can lift him up.

—Ecclesiastes 4:9-10

Contents

For the friends who've changed us

Taylor and Savannah

Annika and Rachel

London

Emma

Kati Anne and Abigail

Veronica

Kayley

Kaitlyn, Camryn, and Olivia

Abigail

hey FRIEND,

So, you've picked up a devotional about friendship. You may wonder, *Does the Bible have much to say about friendship, anyway?*

Turns out, the Bible has a lot to say about friendship, and it started at the very beginning.

God created Adam and set him in the garden of Eden. There was no one like him. Adam was lonely, so God created Eve. Eve was Adam's wife, but she was also his companion—someone he could relate to, tend the garden with, and walk with God alongside.

Their companionship was just as it was supposed to be at first. Then sin broke their relationship. They felt shame around each other and started playing the blame game almost immediately. They were cursed with hostility between them, and that curse extended to every person born.

Cain murdered Abel; Sarah betrayed Hagar; jealousy brewed between Leah and Rachel; the list goes on. Ever since that first friendship fell apart, people and their sin have been breaking relationship after relationship.

Still, there is an innate longing for companionship with other people. We long for friendship to be what it's *supposed* to be. And, even though sin broke our relationships with God and one another, God didn't do away with friendship.

When He sent Adam and Eve out of the garden, He sent them together. When God called Abram to follow Him to a new land, Abram brought his nephew Lot along. The Lord called Aaron to help Moses complete the mission of bringing the Israelites out of slavery and into the promised land. The Bible tells the story of David and his best friend Jonathan, who encouraged David when he was running for his life.

When God the Son came into the world as a human, He chose to walk the earth in intimate friendship with twelve other men. Eleven of those same men went out together to share the gospel and build the church after Jesus ascended to heaven. The epistles—letters written by some of Jesus's disciples—are mostly written to communities of people following Jesus *together*. And when believers are with Jesus for eternity, we will worship Him *together*. Our relationships with God and one another will once again be exactly what they are supposed to be.

But what about now? What are we to do with our friendships that remain broken because of sin? How do we build and keep real and good friendships with one another?

In this devotional, we will look at what God has to say about being friends on this side of heaven. We will read the Bible's stories of friends, warnings for friends, encouragement for friends, and directions for friends. No matter what your friendships look like right now, this devotional is for you.

It's for the friend who is looking for friends.

The one whose friendships feel shallow.

The girl who has been abandoned.

The envious friend.

The friend who has an abundance of friends and still wants more.

The one who needs to end a friendship.

The girl who feels unsatisfied in her friendships.

Each devotion was written by girls who have been (or are) in your shoes right now. Each writer has walked with Jesus alongside friends. They live in different cities, come from different families, have worshipped in different denominations, and are living in different life stages. Some are in college, some are single, some are married, one is engaged at the time of writing, some are moms, some have been Christians their whole lives, and some started following Jesus recently.

Like you, they have been helped by friends and hurt by friends. They have seen what friendship is and what it isn't. They'll show you that friendship isn't mostly about happiness, though it can bring great joy. It isn't mostly about codependency, though it can give us people to lean on. They will remind you that though best friends won't always last our whole lives, the friendships between Jesus-followers will endure eternally. They will help you see that friendship is about sanctifying us—making us more like Jesus—and giving us people to follow God alongside.

Like everything else, friendship will one day be exactly as it was always supposed to be—like it was at the beginning. Except this time, it'll be better.

If I take offense easily;
if I am content to continue in
cold unfriendliness, though
friendship be possible, then I
know nothing of Calvary love.

—Amy Carmichael

WHERE IT BEGAN
Our God Is a God
of Friendship

I was five years old when my mom snapped a picture that lives rent-free inside my head.

My best friend Kelsey had recently moved across the country. For months, I missed her, and I longed to be close to her again. I was giddy the first time my mom took me to see my friend and her family after the big move. You can see joy written all over my face in the picture. We were sitting side-by-side on a couch. I was nestled next to her, arms wrapped around her slender shoulders, lips planted on the side of her face in the most passionate five-year-old kiss you can imagine.

There's only one problem.

While my lips curled into a puckered-up smile squished into my friend's face, hers formed a straight line. While my arms squeezed her body as if they might never let go, hers were immovable boards plastered to her side.

Kelsey and I have laughed about that picture for decades, but I have always felt a little embarrassed by what that picture communicates about me.

Am I desperate for friendship—pathetic even?

I've never been able to deny it: my heart aches for friends. It is written on my heart, and it is written all over my face and body language in that picture. The longing followed me to three different schools in three years of middle and high school. It stayed with me when I was thrust into a new community in college, when I moved to a different city for the first time, and in every changing stage of my life.

While that longing may have made me feel awkward and embarrassed at times, it was never pathetic. It points me to one way I reflect my Creator.

Read Genesis 1-2 and John 17:1-5 and then check out the verses below.

Then God said, "Let us make man in our image, according to our likeness. They will rule the fish of the sea, the birds of the sky, the livestock, the whole earth, and the creatures that crawl on the earth."
So God created man
in his own image;
he created him in the image of God;
he created them male and female.
—Genesis 1:26–27

Our God is a God of friendship, and He created people for friendship too.

Look at the pronouns used in these two verses: *us, our, his,* and *he.*

Moses, the writer of Genesis, wanted the original readers to know there is one God. He used singular pronouns like "he" to describe the Creator. But if God is one God, why does He also describe Himself with words like "us" and "ours" in verse 26?

This is one of the first places in the Bible where God reveals Himself as a Trinity. Through the rest of Scripture's pages, He makes Himself known as three Persons in one God: God the Father, God the Son, and God the Holy Spirit.

Our God is a God of friendship, and He created people for friendship too.

Yet for us there is one God, the Father. All things are from him. (1 Corinthians 8:6)

For to us a child is born, to us a son [Jesus] is given; and the government shall be upon his shoulder, and his name shall be called Wonderful Counselor, Mighty God. (Isaiah 9:6 ESV)

"But when the Helper comes, whom I will send to you from the Father, the Spirit of truth, who proceeds from the Father, he will bear witness about me." (John 15:26 ESV)

"Go therefore and make disciples of all nations, baptizing them in the name of the Father and of the Son and of the Holy Spirit." (Matthew 28:19 ESV)

Since before God created the world, He has been a God of friendship. He had perfect community within Himself as the Trinity, which means He is both three Persons and one God. God created everything and everyone from an overflow of love. Before God created skies and seas, fish and birds, light and darkness, He loved. The Father loved the Son and the Holy Spirit, the Holy Spirit loved the Father and the Son, and the Son loved the Spirit and the Father. Jesus affirms this when He prays in John 17:24, "Father . . . you loved me before the world's foundation."

LET'S CHAT

Genesis 1:27 reveals that God created us in His image. Friends, that means our longing for friendship comes from the God who created us to be like Him.

Our hearts want community because we were made to reflect a God *whose nature* is community. He created us for friendship with Himself, and He created us for friendship with other people.

When we are tempted to believe we don't need anyone other than ourselves, let's remember we were made by a God who is three-in-one. Should we be tempted to feel pathetic in our longing to be known and loved by someone else, let's remember that God Himself etched that longing into our hearts.

If you look at the picture of my best friend and me, you'll see two little girls who needed and wanted friendship in their lives. Those girls didn't yet know where that desire came from, but it already lived in their bones. It was innate. God created people to be together.

Your desire for friendship might look like mine or it might look like my friend's. It may be out on display for the world to see or hidden and kept close to your heart. Over the next thirty days, we will open God's Word together and see His design for friendship. We will see examples of beautiful friendships, and we will see examples of broken friendships. We will challenge our culture's expectations of friendship and learn how to find joy in friendship. We will seek to forgive, pray for, and stick close to our communities.

When we do friendship well here on earth, we reflect the God of heaven.

Our hearts want community because we were made to reflect a God whose nature is community.

WHAT ABOUT YOU?

What are some insecurities you have when it comes to friendship?

_____

_____

_____

_____

_____

_____

What does your community look like right now?

_____

_____

_____

_____

_____

_____

_____

How does knowing that God is a God of community change the way you think about your friendships?

_____

_____

_____

_____

_____

_____

JOURNAL YOUR PRAYERS

Thank God for being a God of community. Praise Him for being a God who has been loving since before the foundation of the world.

_____

_____

_____

_____

_____

_____

_____

_____

_____

Ask God to show you where you need friendship in your life. Pray that He will provide friends who point you to Him.

_____

_____

_____

_____

_____

_____

_____

Confess any feeling of self-reliance. Acknowledge that God created you to have friendship with Himself and with other people. Ask Him to help you believe that.

TAKE IT FURTHER TODAY

Grab a Bible concordance and find references for the word *friend*.
Read those passages to prepare your heart for this devotional.

Text a friend and tell her why you are grateful for her friendship.

Create a screen saver on your phone that says "God is love" to remind yourself
that before God created anything else, He was the God of love.

CRAVING COMMUNITY

People Were Made
for Each Other

Cambria Joy

I don't know about you, but I have experienced seasons of overwhelming loneliness. It's the worst.

For me, nothing quite beats moving to a new town right before my freshman year of high school. My friends told me we'd stay close. We had been in each other's inner circles since third grade. But once the distance between us grew, our friendships shrunk in depth. Texts and phone calls never compare to middle-school hallways, car rides, and sleepovers.

Meanwhile, I knew no one in my new town. I was the new girl, and there was no warm welcome. I felt so alone that I even cried during lunch one day (which made me feel even more pathetic), my hot and fast tears making their great escape before I could hold them back. I was surrounded by people, reminding me just how lonely I was and how I wished I had my friends from back in my hometown. In my new life, my inner circle was empty. There was no circle at all.

When I wanted to forget my loneliness, I discovered a whole new world of connection on the internet. YouTube became my escape, a haven from school, and a place where I found connections and a creative outlet as I fostered a virtual community. Still, my heart craved *physical* community. Although my group of friends on the internet became wide, it didn't go deep. I still felt alone because I wanted to do more than "like" photos of my friends. I wanted to take photos with them.

At a church I visited, the youth pastor preached on how God wired us for connection, that we weren't created to go at life alone. Though it wasn't my choice, that's exactly what I was: alone. I wondered, Is *God disappointed in me because I don't have someone to call "friend"?*

What was I going to do?

Read Genesis 2:15-25
and then check out the verses below.

The man gave names to all the livestock, to the birds of the sky, and to every wild animal; but for the man no helper was found corresponding to him. So the Lord God caused a deep sleep to come over the man, and he slept. God took one of his ribs and closed the flesh at that place. Then the Lord God made the rib he had taken from the man into a woman and brought her to the man.
—Genesis 2:20-22

When God created people in His image, He wove within us a craving for community.

We crave community with God and with people who bear His image. We see it in the very beginning, in Genesis. When God created Adam and asked him to name every animal, Adam wasn't content just hanging out with the monkeys and giraffes. Adam's heart longed for *someone*. Without skipping a beat, God put Adam to sleep in the garden shade and gave Adam someone his heart would soon skip a beat for.

Adam couldn't find what he longed for on his own because it wasn't there.

Our hearts are hardwired for human connection—image-bearing connection. Connection with God and connection with others, whom He has created in His image. Being made in God's image means that we are, in essence, little mirrors of Him.

There was no other image bearer in the garden that day. It was just Adam. That's why Eve represented something much deeper than a romantic lover; she was the physical expression of image-bearing, human connection.

And that, my friend, is a gift from God's heart. He is a God of community, and, because we are made in His image, we are people who crave community. We were created to love God, to be loved by God, and to experience His love alongside other people.

LET'S CHAT

So, what about me—the girl who cried alone at lunch? What about the girl growing up in a digital world who feels discouraged? She's not alone in the garden of Eden waiting for the second human to be created—she's surrounded by billions of humans, unable to connect with one.

God sees you. He knows your loneliness before you do. Even before Adam could bring up his desire from his heart and out of his lips, God saw it wasn't good for him to be alone. Look what God said before Adam couldn't find a helper fit for him:

> God can use loneliness to bring us closer to Him.

When God created people in His image, He wove within us a craving for community.

The Lord God said, "It is not good for the man to be alone. I will make a helper corresponding to him" (Genesis 2:18).

God knows our desires. He can use loneliness to bring us closer to Him. During my season of overwhelming loneliness, my friendship with God deepened. In the soil of solitude, the God who created the farthest, most desolate part of outer space never left me alone. In your season of loneliness, fall into friendship with our Maker. Trust Him to bring friends who will sharpen you to become more like Himself.

Our craving for community shows us one way we are like Him. Your heart desires friendship because God placed that desire in there. He will be in our circle, always—from now into eternity. Jesus is our friend who doesn't just walk beside us; His Spirit dwells in us. He is with us, in every sense of the word, now and forever.

Read Psalm 145:19. Describe how wonderful it is that God knows your needs before you tell them to Him. How does this shape your understanding of God's gift of friendship?

What do you desire right now when it comes to friendship?

How does knowing that God wants to give you the gift of friendship change your view of friendship?

JOURNAL YOUR PRAYERS

Thank God that He is a forever friend. Praise Him for being a faithful friend, even when you are not.

_____

_____

_____

_____

_____

_____

_____

_____

_____

Ask God to bring the right friends into your life—friends who will sharpen you and shape you into a person who looks more like Jesus.

_____

_____

_____

_____

Confess your desire for godly friends to God and surrender the timeline to His hands.

TAKE IT FURTHER TODAY

Do more than show up to church—get involved in a Bible study
and get plugged into your local church community.

Be open to receiving the friends God has for you,
and don't be afraid to get vulnerable with new friends.

Open your home if you can. Host a girls' Bible study
or a gathering a couple of times a month in your space.
Cultivate community in the soil God has given you.

Alena T.

BOUND *NOT* TO BREAK

How Friends Help Us Obey God

Growing up, I always had godly people around me. I am what some people might call straitlaced, maybe even uptight. If my mom were here, she'd laugh and tell you she never had to convince me to get good grades. That was a pressure I placed on myself—starting in kindergarten. (If I could go back, I'd tell little-girl Lena to loosen up a bit.)

I went from one small Christian school to the next, depending on where we lived. I don't remember a school year when I wasn't surrounded by friends and family who loved Jesus and spurred me on to love Him too.

When I graduated high school, I found myself in a new city, with new surroundings, and zero Jesus-loving friends or family. I didn't notice at first, but the longer I went without godly community, the quieter the voice of God became—not because He stopped talking to me but because I stopped listening.

One night, I found myself on a college campus, at a local party, surrounded by everything except Jesus. It was dark, and the place reeked of liquor and other rancid smells. The large room was bursting with people, yet it felt empty. I had a chilling realization: "No one in here cares about my relationship with God."

It was the first time I realized that I was bound to break without godly community.

Read Hebrews 3:12-15; 10:19-39 and then check out the verse below.

And let us consider how we may spur one another on toward love and good deeds. —Hebrews 10:24 NIV

Godly friendship leads to godly obedience.

We aren't supposed to follow God alone. Scripture repeatedly teaches about the importance of godly community, and Hebrews 10:19-39 makes this crystal clear. Verses 19-23 reveal that Jesus's followers get to draw near to God because of Jesus's death and resurrection. Then Hebrews 3:12-15 and 10:24-25 show the importance of walking through life with fellow followers of Jesus. These are the people who will encourage us to *keep drawing close to God* and remind us that *He is better than anything else.*

Following Jesus in a world that doesn't love Him is hard, but the joy that comes from doing it with friends makes it a whole lot easier. And, God doesn't merely suggest we seek godly friendships. He commands it.

GODLY FRIENDSHIP LEADS TO GODLY OBEDIENCE.

Hebrews 10:26 addresses what happens when we are disobedient, when we "neglect to gather together." It becomes easier to live a life of disobedience when we lack Jesus-following friendships. When we don't surround ourselves with godly community, we deliberately open ourselves up to temptation and, eventually, sin.

The reverse is true too: godly friendship leads to accountability, and accountability leads us to obey God. Godly friends will remind you of God's grace and urge you to walk in love and obedience to God.

LET'S CHAT

As believers in Jesus, we must pursue friendship with fellow believers. It is hard to hear the voice of God without a community encouraging you to listen. You know what's even harder? Obeying the voice of God when no one is encouraging you to obey.

First things first: find and plug into a local church. I'm not talking about ducking in and out of service once a week. The writer of Hebrews reminds followers of Jesus that they need to live in community with and encourage one another regularly.

For some of us, finding godly friendship is easy. Maybe it looks like plugging into your local church's small group or joining that Bible club at your school. But maybe you are more like I was when I moved away from my Christian friends. You

God doesn't merely suggest we seek out godly friendships. He commands it.

are in a new environment, and finding godly friendship feels like the hardest task of your life. Or maybe you come from a family that doesn't know Jesus, and it feels like everywhere you turn there is darkness. You think that no one would want to join you in your pursuit of Christ.

My encouragement is to pray. Get on your knees and ask our gracious and compassionate God to send you friends who know and love Him. I can attest that He *will* send them in His timing.

I made a big move the summer before my freshman year of high school. I left behind all my closest friends, and I remember begging God for friends as good as the ones I'd had

Get on your knees and ask our gracious and compassionate God to send you friends who know and love Him.

before. He didn't send me twenty, and He didn't send them in the way I asked. But He did send one.

My dad (who was a recent widower after my mom's death) befriended a fellow widow and her new husband, and we had dinner together. They had a daughter my age. She was chatty, and I was very shy and reserved at the time. She simply pursued me. I pushed back for a while. But as she stayed, my trust in her grew. To this day, she is a constant voice of godly reason and love to me.

We need godly friendships. We need people who will point us to the cross. We were created for community, and seeking out a godly community leads to lives of obedience that point to Jesus.

WHAT ABOUT YOU?

Do you have friends who are pursuing Christ alongside you? How do you follow Him together?

_____

_____

_____

_____

_____

Describe how your friends encourage you to obey God. If they don't, how would you like them to?

_____

_____

_____

_____

What does it look like to be a godly friend?

_____

_____

_____

_____

_____

JOURNAL YOUR PRAYERS

Thank God for being a God of community. Praise Him for being a God who did not create us to live in isolation but to walk in the light with others.

Ask God to send friendships your way that honor and glorify Him. Pray that He will send friends who will spur you on in love and obedience to Him.

Confess any ways in which you have not embodied Hebrews 10:24 in your friendships.

TAKE IT FURTHER TODAY

Get plugged into a local church. Join a community group.

Be brave! Don't be afraid to be vulnerable and honest
about the fact that you're looking for godly friends.

Pray. Write a prayer on your mirror in dry-erase marker
so that you will remember to ask God daily
to provide godly friendships.

Alexus Lee

BEARING BURDENS
Why We Need Friends with Faith

When I graduated high school, I had high hopes of being like all the other girls I knew—getting into university, moving away from home, finding new friends, and starting fresh. But while all my friends got into their dream schools, I did not get into *any* of the universities I applied to.

Not one.

I stayed home and went to community college. It felt like my worst nightmare. I wouldn't know anyone because everyone else was leaving.

Not to be dramatic, but it felt like my life was over.

So, I embarked on a season of loneliness. And sulking. Lots of sulking. I half-heartedly asked God to help me trust Him and find friends while I was in this place I didn't want to be. I got tired of praying the same prayers day after day. I also got tired of watching other girls on Instagram make tons of friends in their dorms on their beautiful campuses. I found myself growing spiritually weary. Could God actually be working in my life? Or had He abandoned me?

One day, one of my older friends and mentors, Nena, reached out. She told me she understood my sadness. She said she was "carrying the weight of my belief." She was carrying my burdens too, and she wanted to help me get out of my season of spiritual weakness. Though I felt spiritually weak, she was and had been strong—praying and believing on my behalf that God was going to provide a community that spurred me toward Jesus.

For the first time since I began community college, I felt like God was listening. It was like God said, "Daughter, I see you. I know it has been hard for you, but do not give up." The encouragement I felt in knowing that someone else was praying and believing God for me when I felt too weak to do it on my own brought overwhelming peace.

Read Luke 5:17-26
and then check out the verse below.

Carry one another's burdens; in this way you will fulfill the law of Christ.—Galatians 6:2

The best kind of friend will carry our burdens. They will have faith in God even when we don't.

Luke 5 shows us the power of friends' faith. During Jesus's ministry, He made a reputation for traveling around, teaching about God, and healing people. One group of people had a friend who was paralyzed. He couldn't go to Jesus to be healed on his own. While Jesus was in their town, the group got together and carried their friend to Jesus. When they couldn't get through the door of the building where Jesus was teaching, they cut a hole in the roof to lower him down! We can't know the exact state of the paralyzed man's heart, but we can see that his friends' faith

The best kind of friend will carry our burdens. They will have faith in God even when we don't.

grabbed Jesus's attention. These friends believed Jesus could provide forgiveness, healing, and mercy. Their belief changed their friend's world forever.

Their faith made them willing to go to great lengths for the well-being of their friend (I mean, they cut a hole in someone's roof!) and led them to a place they couldn't imagine in their wildest dreams. In their limited view, they saw their friend needed physical healing, but Jesus saw what he needed most: the forgiveness of his sin.

Their faith became a witness to everyone else. Luke 5:26 says, "Then everyone was astounded, and they were giving glory to God. And they were filled with awe and said, 'We have seen incredible things today.'"

ur friends' faith can significantly impact our lives. When we are spiritually weak, when we feel like we can't walk to the throne of God on our own, we need friends who will carry us there—who will go to lengths we could never imagine to take us to Jesus.

JESUS SAW WHAT HE TRULY NEEDED.

LET'S CHAT

Being a friend and finding friends who are people of faith is essential.

We've got to ask ourselves: *What do my friends believe? Do my friends have faith that will carry me when I'm weak?*

> We need friends
> who know God's
> Word and will
> speak it over us.

We can also ask, *Am I that kind of friend to others?*

Nena believed on my behalf. Not only did she believe God was working for me, but Nena also helped me to act when I wanted to keep sulking. About a week after our conversation, Nena helped me plug into a local college ministry. God answered her prayers that I would find community with a resounding yes. When I trusted Him again, I found friendships that changed my life forever.

Nena prayed for me and carried my burdens. Then she physically brought me to be with God's people at a campus ministry. During seasons of weakness, our friends—like my friend Nena—come alongside us. Their faith allows them to love us as themselves.

We need friends who know God's Word and will speak it over us, who have thriving prayer lives, who will bring our burdens to God, and who love the church and will encourage us to be in community with God's people.

The friends in Luke 5 had faith in the living God. Because of that, their friend was healed in more ways than they could fathom.

WHAT ABOUT YOU?

What areas of your life feel spiritually weak?

Which friends in your life can you ask to pray for and encourage you?

Which friends do you know who might be spiritually weak? How can you help carry that friend's burden?

JOURNAL YOUR PRAYERS

Thank God that in times when you have struggled to trust Him, He knew exactly what people and friends needed to be in your life.

_____

_____

_____

_____

_____

_____

_____

_____

_____

_____

_____

Ask God to reveal which friends may need your help to trust in Him.

_____

_____

_____

_____

_____

_____

_____

Confess any areas in your life where you know that your friendships are not glorifying God and ask God to provide healthy, faithful friends.

TAKE IT FURTHER TODAY

Schedule time to talk with one to two friends about ways
you are struggling and growing in your faith.

Check up on one another's strengths and weaknesses
when you meet together.

Pray with and for your friends in random moments.
(This is a game-changer!)

FULL OF JOY

If you were to ask me what things are essential for a girls' night in, I'd quickly answer:

Dessert

Comfy clothes

A movie with some *DRAMA*

It doesn't have to be a movie either. Whether it's a romantic comedy, a thriller book, reality TV, you name it, I love anything that keeps me on the edge of my seat. If it has a plot with angst and tension, I'm in! Here's the general premise:

The protagonist, or the main character, is the person the audience is most invested in. On the flip side, the antagonist—or villain—creates tension through their interactions with the main character. Someone did someone else dirty, someone wants to get revenge, you get the idea. The next thing you know, there is a journey of back and forth, a game of tug-of-war, until a resolution comes. Or better yet—you're left with a cliffhanger. Friends, this is drama at its finest!

But do you know what's drama at its worst? Experiencing it with real-life people.

Whether it's a miscommunication, a friend gossiping about you, a friend ghosting you when you needed them to show up, or a friend who leaves you more exhausted than encouraged, friendships wrapped in drama can be defeating. Often, it feels easier to avoid the "villains" than to face them. But navigating drama and tension in friendship isn't new. The Bible has words of wisdom to help us through it.

Read Philippians 4:1–9
and then check out the verses below.

Always be full of joy in the Lord. I say it again—rejoice! Let everyone see that you are considerate in all you do. Remember, the Lord is coming soon. Don't worry about anything; instead, pray about everything. Tell God what you need, and thank him for all he has done.—Philippians 4:4–6 NLT

Sometimes we are called to endure difficulty in friendships for the joy of the Lord.

Paul, a man God chose to spread the good news of Jesus, wrote a letter to the Philippian church, urging people to fight for unity with one another. In the fourth chapter, he addressed two women in the church who had tension between them. Whatever disagreement they had affected not only these two women but also the whole church. The conflict between Euodia and Syntyche caused a division that led to isolation and separation. Yet Paul urged the church to shift their perspective from fighting against one another to fighting *for* friendship.

Sometimes we are called to endure difficulty in friendships for the joy of the Lord.

Instead of taking sides and sinking further into division, Paul asked the women to settle their disagreement because they were unified in the most important thing: they belonged to God. These two women had the same heavenly Father. They both mirrored the image of God. They followed Jesus and were filled with His Spirit. Belonging to God means that disagreements between Christians aren't "me vs. you" but "us vs. the problem."

As followers of Jesus, we don't fight against each other—we fight *for* each other.

Paul reminded the Philippians that in fighting for friendship, they must be full of joy in the Lord. We are to be full of joy too. Overflowing joy in God allows us to be so focused on Him that things like little disagreements, the areas where we differ, or even drama that could divide us don't take our focus off Him.

We all have different upbringings, backgrounds, and histories. That's okay—it's even a good thing! We were never created to be the same. We were created to be unified. We were created to be one team that works together for the glory of God.

LET'S CHAT

The danger in viewing people as antagonists in our "dramas" is that we begin to treat them as "villains" instead of as sisters or brothers. It's easy to believe that when we disagree with a friend or tension arises, we should cut off or cancel that friend. Don't we see it in the drama we watch and read? It's often much easier to push people away and separate yourself altogether.

Yet God has given us tools to navigate conflict. The Holy Spirit is our ultimate guide in mending relationships we may view as broken and irredeemable. The Bible shows us that we aren't the first to deal with sin and drama in our friendships.

One way I navigate tension in friendships is by thinking through four P's:

1) *PAUSE:* Be still and listen. Ask yourself, *What narratives am I believing about the other person/myself? What is making me upset right now?* (James 1:19)

2) *PRAY:* Let God in. Ask yourself, *What do I need to surrender that I'm carrying? What does God have that I need?* Take time to pray for yourself and the other person. (Philippians 4:6)

3) *PREPARE:* Study the pathway of Jesus. Take time to read through the life and the person of Jesus. Abide in Him. Ask Him to show you how He would have handled this situation when He was navigating relationships in His life. (Hebrews 4:15)

4) *PROCEED:* Take steps forward. Ask the friend to have a conversation and address the disagreement head-on. Acknowledge what happened and extend grace and forgiveness. (1 Peter 4:8)

Keep pausing.
Keep praying.
Keep preparing.
Keep proceeding in love.

I've had moments when I've believed a friend was truly against me because of a miscommunication. It was easy to create my own narrative of what they thought, assume things about how they viewed me, or follow a thought pattern that simply wasn't true. But when I focused on finding joy in the Lord, fighting for unity instead of drama was much easier.

Sometimes your fight for unity will be successful, and sometimes your friends won't be interested. Keep pausing. Keep praying. Keep preparing. Keep proceeding in love.

Don't be mistaken—fighting for friendship isn't easy. Fighting not to believe false narratives, fighting to remain level-headed, and fighting not to continually bring up the past is tough and grueling work. But the joy of the Lord is way better than the movies—no drama attached!

WHAT ABOUT YOU?

How do you typically respond when conflict arises in friendships?

How does belonging to the Lord change your response to tension?

In what situation in your life do you need God's peace to guard your heart and mind? Pray for that situation.

JOURNAL YOUR PRAYERS

Thank God for security in Him. In God, we can stand strong even in disagreements and tensions that may shake us.

_____

_____

_____

_____

_____

_____

_____

_____

_____

Ask God to reveal ways you naturally react to drama in friendships. Whether you run, avoid, or fight back, ask God to help you be more like Him.

_____

_____

_____

_____

_____

Acknowledge areas of hurt in any current or past friendships.
Confess to the Lord ways you have hurt others and ask for wisdom
to navigate reconciliation and/or healing.

TAKE IT FURTHER TODAY

If you feel drama starting to form in your
friendships, defuse the situation by offering to pray for unity.

Find an older Christian woman in your life and ask her to pray for you
and counsel you when you are dealing with drama in friendships.

Create a worship playlist that makes you feel joyful and listen to that
playlist often—especially when you are navigating drama.

WISHING TO
BE FRIENDS IS
QUICK WORK, BUT
FRIENDSHIP IS A
SLOW-RIPENING
FRUIT.

—Aristotle

CHRIST IS EVERYTHING

Finding Identity in Jesus Instead of Friends

Gabrielle McCullough

For most of my childhood, I had this one *best* friend. We were locked at the hip. We met in kindergarten and were inseparable. I remember thinking we would be friends forever—college roommates, bridesmaids at each other's weddings, and mom friends having playdates with our future kids. She meant the world to me.

Being her friend made me feel significant—even worthy. If we were on good terms, my life would be great. If we weren't on good terms—not so much. My confidence ebbed and flowed based on what she thought of me.

During my freshman year of high school, I found out that I hadn't been invited to my best friend's birthday party. I was devastated. Up to that point, we had spent every birthday together. I was in shock. I felt like I had been punched in the gut and stabbed in the back at the same time. I felt alone, confused, and shattered. *Did I do something wrong? Did I not do enough to earn her friendship?* I came home from school that day and, when I saw my mom, I cried immediately.

She looked at me, wiped the tears off my face, and said, "I know it might feel like you have *nothing* right now, but because you have Jesus, you actually have *everything.*"

Read Ephesians 2:1–10
and then check out the verses below.

For by grace you have been saved through faith. And this is not your own doing; it is the gift of God, not a result of works, so that no one may boast.—Ephesians 2:8–9 ESV

Our identities are found in Jesus—not friendship.

Paul, the author of Ephesians, reminded the church in Ephesus that every area of their lives was marked by their new identity in Jesus.

All of us are tempted to love the things of this world more than we love God. We often are obsessed with appearance, pleasure, success, and even *friendships*. We look to these things to find satisfaction, but we're left empty because these things never last. Friends can come and go, success feels good only for a moment, and our appearance changes. Our hearts long to be filled by something that lasts forever. This satisfaction can only be found in Jesus. Because of Jesus, we have access to something far greater than all these things combined.

OUR IDENTITIES ARE FOUND IN JESUS— NOT FRIENDSHIP.

Jesus died on the cross and rose from the grave to forgive our sins and offer us salvation. That's the best news ever! It is because of this gift, which we have received by grace through faith, that we can stop looking to the world to find our identity. We look to Jesus for our identity. While the things of this world come and go, His love remains the same. We can be secure in our identity. He will never leave us, and He will never let us down.

God created His people to know Him and worship Him for all our days (Ephesians 2:10). We have worth because we have been created by a worthy God. We are loved because Jesus Christ took on flesh and paid for our sin so that we don't have to.

Who or what sits on the throne of your heart? Is Jesus truly the Lord of your life—the one who holds your identity? Or have you allowed friendships or your social status to take His place?

LET'S CHAT

In my freshman year of high school, I placed my identity in a friendship. It was a foundation that wasn't secure. I found my significance in someone who could (and did) let me down. When the foundation began to crack, I felt like my worthiness would be destroyed.

The reality is, your friends cannot save you, your appearance cannot save you, and your success cannot save you. Only Jesus can.

We can be secure in our identity.

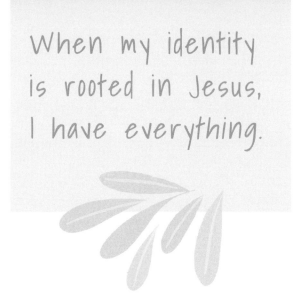

When my identity is rooted in Jesus, I have everything.

My mom's encouragement that day was profound. When my identity is rooted in Jesus, I have everything. My identity is secure in Him. He will never let me down. Psalm 16:11 says, "You make known to me the path of life; in your presence there is fullness of joy; at your right hand are pleasures forevermore" (ESV). Every time we place our identity in anything or anyone other than Christ, we are left feeling empty and unsatisfied. Only He can fully quench our longing to be loved, seen, and known. He is where everlasting joy and pleasure are found!

Let's quit measuring our worth by what our friends think of us, and instead measure our worth by what the Creator of the universe thinks. He says you are His masterpiece (Ephesians 2:10 NLT)! When you feel like you are on the outskirts of a friendship like I did my freshman year, remind yourself that the King of heaven and earth has invited you into the inner circle of His presence for eternity. When you feel like you must work hard to keep your friendships, remind yourself that God has saved you by grace—you don't have to work hard to have a friendship with Him.

When you feel like you have *nothing*, remind yourself that, because you have Jesus, you actually have *everything*.

WHAT ABOUT YOU?

In what ways have you placed your identity or worth in your friendships rather than in Christ?

_____

_____

_____

_____

_____

To whom or what do you look to find satisfaction?

_____

_____

_____

_____

_____

How does knowing you have been created by God and for God impact your identity and confidence?

_____

_____

_____

_____

_____

JOURNAL YOUR PRAYERS

Reflect on a time when you felt hurt by a friend. Did you allow that to impact your value and worth? Why or why not?

_____

_____

_____

_____

_____

_____

_____

_____

_____

Spend some time asking God to reveal where you are prone to pursue satisfaction and pleasure outside of Him. Then confess those things and ask for forgiveness.

_____

_____

_____

_____

_____

_____

Ask God to reveal the unique good works He has planned and prepared for you. Ask Him to give you the boldness and faith to obey all He has called you to do.

TAKE IT FURTHER TODAY

Consider which friendships you find your identity in. This week,
make a plan to spend more time with God than you do with that friend.

Start every day by studying God's Word.

Memorize Psalm 16:11 to remind yourself who holds your identity.

EVERYTHING IN COMMON

Finding Friendship in the Church

Lauren Graves

I'm ready to turn the corner into the room when I hear voices. Friends are shouting as they see each other for the first time after a long summer. They squeal; they laugh; they remind me I am new to this crowd, my new collegiate speech and debate team. It's even more jarring when I see them.

Smiles are plastered across their faces, showing me that they know one another. I don't know a soul.

I start the awkward dance of introducing myself. "Hi, I'm Lauren. Yes, I'm a freshman. Nice to meet you too." *I am possibly the most awkward person on the planet—definitely the most awkward in this room.*

I spy a girl who looks about my age. "Hey, are you a freshman too?"

"Yes," she breathes out in relief.

We ask get-to-know-you questions, but this time, something is different. It's like we already know one another. The next hour is spent hearing about everyone's summers, learning forty-five new names, and wondering whether joining a college speech team was a good life choice or not. My new friend Taylor and I never leave each other's side.

At the end of the meeting, we start the long trek back to the freshman dorms.

"What did you do this summer?" she asks.

"Not much. I said goodbye to my friends before we went our separate ways, got ready to join the team, and went to camp with my church."

Taylor stops. "You're a Christian too?"

> Read Acts 2
> and then check out the verses below.
>
> *Now all the believers were together and held all things in common. They sold their possessions and property and distributed the proceeds to all, as any had need. Every day they devoted themselves to meeting together in the temple, and broke bread from house to house.* —Acts 2:44-46

Christian friendship is different than any other kind of friendship.

Acts 2 is the first description we have of the early church, and it's one of the Bible's most important pictures of friendship. After Jesus ascended to heaven, the Holy Spirit came to dwell in Jesus's followers. In one day, thousands of people came to believe in Jesus! Most of these people had little in common. They were from different cities, spoke different languages, came from different religions, and probably spanned every part of the economic spectrum. But once they became Christians, everything changed.

Christian friendship is different than any other kind of friendship.

Suddenly, they had the most important thing in common. Ephesians 2:13 reminds us that all believers were once far away from Christ, but because of His blood, we have been brought near to Him. Our unity doesn't come from our neighborhoods, generations, skin colors, political parties, or anything else that may make us feel unified. Our unity comes from Jesus.

The early church's unity led them to sacrifice for one another. They sold their possessions for one another, and they gave their time, talents, and resources to each other. They loved each other in spirit and action in ways that may seem extreme, but their sacrificial generosity allowed them to follow Jesus together in a culture that didn't make that easy.

They also devoted themselves to following God *together*. These new Christians knew that following God together is far better than following Him alone. They followed Him as the global church—all believers across time and location—and local churches—Christians who commit themselves together in a particular time and place.

Being a Christian wasn't the culturally acceptable thing to do in the first century. Christians lost their jobs, their families, and sometimes their lives to follow Jesus. Still, they never had to do it alone. God gave them one another. Together, they devoted their lives to Jesus and the gospel, helping and encouraging each other until their lives on earth were over and they met Jesus face to face.

LET'S CHAT

If you are looking for friendship, look for Christians. The connection believers share is better than any other connection. It's better than living close to someone or connecting on your politics, socioeconomic status, or talents. It's a unifying, sacrificial, devoted kind of connection.

IF YOU ARE LOOKING FOR FRIENDSHIP, LOOK FOR CHRISTIANS.

In difference, Christians find unity in the church (Galatians 3:27–28). In need, we find help in the church, and we can bring help to the church (1 Corinthians 12:4). Most importantly, in our mission of following Jesus and sharing the gospel, Christians find encouragement in the church (Hebrews 10:24–25).

The friendship that began that day with Taylor hasn't yet come to an end. We discovered we were both Christians on a team of people who didn't follow Jesus, and suddenly, *we had the most important thing in common*. It didn't matter that we came from different cities. It didn't matter that we had become Christians in different seasons of our lives. It didn't matter that we grew up in families that didn't resemble one another or that we liked different music or had different skin tones or anything at all. (Though I think we would both say our differences make our friendship better.)

We followed the same Jesus. We shared convictions. We had the same mission.

For a short season, Taylor and I followed Jesus side-by-side. But soon enough, we retreated to our separate cities, having tasted the goodness of God in our friendship, and threw ourselves into local churches.

My friendship with Taylor felt serendipitous. How lucky that on our college speech team, where Christians were few and far between, we would meet one another. But Acts 2 reminds us that there was nothing lucky about it. God means for Christians to have one another. He gave us *the church* to find friendships that are different—better—than any other friendships on earth.

WHAT ABOUT YOU?

Do you feel like you have more in common with other believers than unbelievers? Why?

_____

_____

_____

_____

What are some ways you can make sacrifices for the Christians in your life?

_____

_____

_____

_____

What do you think it looks like to devote yourself to other Christians?

_____

_____

_____

_____

_____

JOURNAL YOUR PRAYERS

Praise God for the global and local church. Thank Him for the Christians He has placed in your life.

_____

_____

_____

_____

_____

_____

_____

_____

_____

_____

_____

Confess any way you have gossiped about or belittled people in the church, both locally and globally.

_____

_____

_____

_____

_____

Ask God to make your heart warm to the Christians at your local church, in your community, and around the world.

TAKE IT FURTHER TODAY

If you don't have a local church, make a list of five churches you can visit.
If you do have a local church, list five ways you can get more involved.

Talk about God or church at work, school, or any place where there aren't many
Christians. You never know when you'll find a new believer to connect with.

Go to your church leadership and ask where they need people to serve.
Serve where you are needed, even if it's not something you'd choose to do.
You'll often make friends as you serve with other believers.

Tara Sun

WHEREVER YOU GO
The Cost of Friendship

I'm sure you've heard it said before: "I'll scratch your back if you scratch mine." Or maybe, "Relationships are 50/50."

It's true—some friendships are perfectly equal and mutually beneficial. But now and again, a friendship isn't quite so simple.

Confession: Friendship has never been easy for me. It comes with struggles that often lead me to desperately cling to any friendship I have. When I was in the sixth grade, I went to a tiny Christian school where I was the only girl in my middle school class. After what felt like an eternity, a new student enrolled; lo and behold, *it was a girl*.

FINALLY.

I relentlessly pursued a friendship with her by inviting her over to my house, finding every opportunity to play with her at recess, and always arranging our desks next to each other.

But my eager excitement and energy began to fade when I realized what this friendship was costing me. While I made every effort to sit with her at lunch, she moved away or started talking with someone else. When I invited her to my house after school, she was "too busy." My sacrifice felt less than worth it.

"Friendship shouldn't feel this hard," I confessed to God, "...right?"

Read Ruth 1
and then check out the verse below.

*But Ruth said, "Do not urge me to leave you or to return from
following you. For where you go I will go, and where you lodge
I will lodge. Your people shall be my people, and your God my God."*
—Ruth 1:16 ESV

Sometimes God calls us to stick with a friendship even when it doesn't make sense.

The book of Ruth is famously known as a love story between its namesake, Ruth, and a dashing farm boy (well, more like a man) named Boaz. But it's not only a love story. There's a golden thread woven through this book that's easily overlooked: *friendship.*

Put yourself in Ruth's shoes (or sandals). You just lost all the men in your family: your husband, father-in-law, and brother-in-law. In that culture, when a woman's husband died, she was practically ruined. No income. No security. No home. Ruth's options were to either move back home with her parents or stay with her penniless (and maybe even grumpy) mother-in-law, Naomi, who was going to an unknown land with an unplanned plan.

Sometimes God calls us to stick with a friendship even when it doesn't make sense.

For Ruth, there were more reasons to gracefully end the friendship with her mother-in-law than reasons to stay. Naomi even urged her to leave because she had nothing to offer Ruth. She begged Ruth to move on and start anew. Frankly—Naomi had a point.

But Ruth counted the cost and decided to do the unexpected. Ruth clung to Naomi (Ruth 1:14). Even with her husband gone, Ruth's love for her mother-in-law compelled her to remain and pursue a friendship.

Against all odds, Ruth abandoned what made sense, sacrificed quite a lot, and made a covenant with God and Naomi that she would stay (Ruth 1:17). One of the words the Bible uses to describe God's love is *hesed*. It means that God's love is faithful and covenantal. Ruth imitated God's *hesed* with her faithful, committed love to Naomi.

LET'S CHAT

Sometimes, God calls us to stick it out and faithfully pursue a friendship even when it doesn't make sense, costs us more than it blesses us, and feels like we're the only ones contributing.

Why? Because friendship isn't just about us. It's not about what we can gain or how others can fulfill our needs.

Friend, we are called in Christ to be examples of His love. In Luke 9:23, Jesus used the phrase "take up your cross." It means following Jesus may lead to suffering, uncertainty, or discomfort, but it's worth choosing to follow Him anyway.

Ruth imitated God's *hesed* with her faithful, committed love to Naomi.

That's what Jesus did for us when He sacrificed His life on the cross.

Sticking with a hard friendship can feel one-sided, draining, time-consuming, or emotionally exhausting. But if God calls us to remain in that friendship, may we remember we are not alone. God is with us, and we are fighting together. The hardships and sacrifices will all be worth it to become the person God is shaping us into: *someone who looks more like Jesus*.

One quick note: I'm not saying you should stick with a friendship that is abusive or leading you down a path of sin (read more on page 90).

We are called in Christ to be examples of His love.

But when a friendship is simply uncomfortable or inconvenient, we can demonstrate God's faithful and covenantal love (His *hesed*) to others by making the sacrifice, just like Jesus did for us.

What I didn't tell you about my friendship in middle school is that although it was hard, one-sided, and costly, God used it to make me a resilient and faithful friend. It taught me that friendship isn't about how my back can be scratched. It also taught me that people need the love of Christ in friendship, even if they don't realize it or reciprocate right away. Slowly but surely, my friendship with the girl who didn't want anything to do with me changed. Though we didn't become inseparable, the Lord answered my prayer for companionship.

If you are exhausted from giving 110 percent to a friendship that feels costly, remember what friendship with us cost Jesus. He took the punishment for your sins on the cross. Just as we were given faithful and sacrificial love, we can give it to the friends God has placed in our lives.

WHAT ABOUT YOU?

Name a few things that you have had to sacrifice for a friendship. How did you handle it?

How does the faithful, covenant love of God inspire you to be a better friend?

Think of one person you can call, text, or hang out in person with this week. How does taking the first step to initiate show the faithful, constant love of God?

JOURNAL YOUR PRAYERS

Thank God for His faithful and sacrificial love for you. Praise Him for the gift of His Son, who laid down His life for His friends.

_____

_____

_____

_____

_____

_____

_____

_____

_____

_____

Ask God to reveal any areas where you need to build resilience, patience, and faithfulness to become a better friend and witness for Jesus. Ask Him to bring you friends who build you up when other friendships are draining.

_____

_____

_____

_____

_____

Confess any feelings of bitterness, anger, or resentment toward friends. Pray for God to help you forgive them and move forward in peace.

TAKE IT FURTHER TODAY

When you're navigating a draining friendship, make sure to surround yourself with true, life-giving friends and family.

Read 1 Peter 4:8-10 to encourage you to refresh your mind with God's definition of friendship and keep being godly with your friends.

Write down five ways to set a godly example around a difficult friend so that person encounters Jesus every time they see you.

NOT JUST A NUMBER
How Godly Friendships Cross Age Barriers

Joanne Faith Russell

Most people say I'm an old soul.

And I'd say they're right. I love hanging around the older women at my church, my older colleagues, and even my nearly eighty-year-old auntie. So it's no surprise that one of my closest friends is eleven years older than me.

I met Michelle in 2020. At the time, I was lonely, living in my hometown, and suffering from a debilitating shoulder injury that left me unable to do what I love most—dance. (Oh yeah, and there was this little pandemic that left me and the rest of the world feeling extremely isolated.)

Although we hadn't known each other long, Michelle quickly became a much-needed light in my life during a bleak year. We understood each other's humor, supported each other even though we were in different life seasons, and had fun together. Michelle is a busy professional with her own friend group—something I always longed for—but she still made time for me.

I couldn't have made it through the loneliness of the pandemic without her.

I often wondered why this busy woman with her own established life made time for me—someone eleven years her junior who was still learning the ropes of adulthood.

Read 2 Kings 2:1-11
and then check out the verse below.

One generation will declare your works to the next and will proclaim your mighty acts. —Psalm 145:4

Friendships aren't just for people in the same age bracket.

God gives us friends of all different ages and generations so that we can help one another grow spiritually.

In 1 and 2 Kings, we meet a pair of unlikely friends: Elijah and Elisha. Elijah met Elisha soon after one of Elijah's bleakest moments. In 1 Kings 19:4, Elijah was so depressed that he begged God to take his life. Forty days later, God instructed him to anoint Elisha as a prophet in his place. Elijah did as he was told, and their friendship began.

Elijah and Elisha had a mentoring relationship. Elisha followed and served Elijah, who was the older of the two.

By 2 Kings 2, they were getting ready to say goodbye to one another. Elijah and Elisha hadn't spent a lifetime together. The two men worked alongside each other for about two years before this farewell.

FRIENDSHIPS AREN'T JUST FOR PEOPLE IN THE SAME AGE BRACKET.

Still, when God took Elijah away from the earth, Elisha's sadness was evident. He didn't want to leave Elijah, and he mourned losing him (2 Kings: 2:12). In their unique friendship, Elisha was privy to Elijah's experience, wisdom, and knowledge, and he wanted to learn everything he could from Elijah.

But it wasn't just Elisha who gained something from this friendship. Elisha challenged Elijah when he asked for two shares of Elijah's spirit (2 Kings 2:9). Perhaps Elijah thought that Elisha would ask for something smaller, something that was easier for him to give, or something that required less effort.

A double portion of Elijah's spirit was a big request! Even at the very end of Elijah's illustrious ministry, he was challenged by the young prophet he mentored. Elijah's friendship with Elisha caused him to keep growing in his faith until the moment he was taken away by God.

> Elisha wanted to learn everything he could from Elijah.

LET'S CHAT

When friendships cross generations, older friends can serve as mentors, role models, and guides to younger friends, especially those still learning the ropes of life. Our older friends can remind us of ways God remains trustworthy over time and walk us through the "firsts" that they have experienced already.

Similarly, younger friends can stretch and challenge their older friends. Younger friends often think with fewer boundaries and limits. Possibilities seem endless. Our younger friends may challenge us to pray big prayers, have faith that defies logic, and teach us to be less jaded by life and more optimistic about what's possible.

Cross-generational friendships are powerful tools God can use to stretch the older generation and develop the younger ones.

God brought Michelle and me together at just the right time, and our friendship has been a source of joy in my life ever since. I always thought that friends were supposed to be in the same life stage, going through similar experiences at the same time. But God didn't intend for us to have such a limited view of friendship. What a blessing it was to have a friend who had already been where I was!

Big, deep, and meaningful friendships don't always require you to know each other for a long time or even be the same age. You have a lot to offer to someone younger or older than you, so be open to a new friendship with someone of a different generation. Whether your soul is old or young, God may be gifting you a unique friendship outside of your age bracket that you would have never expected.

Big, deep, and meaningful friendships don't always require you to be the same age.

WHAT ABOUT YOU?

Who are some older women in your community you could befriend? What about younger girls?

_____

_____

_____

_____

_____

_____

How could you benefit from having a mentor in your life?

_____

_____

_____

_____

_____

What are some barriers preventing cross-generational friendships in your life, and how can you overcome them?

_____

_____

_____

_____

_____

JOURNAL YOUR PRAYERS

Praise God for the wisdom He gives and the people He provides to share it with us.

_____

_____

_____

_____

_____

_____

_____

_____

_____

_____

_____

Confess when you have rejected wisdom or sound guidance from an older adult. Ask God to help you have a receptive and teachable heart.

_____

_____

_____

_____

Thank God for Christian community. Ask God to use you in a younger girl's life right now, and pray He'll provide seasoned women in your life who can lead you in the right direction.

TAKE IT FURTHER TODAY

Approach older women in your church or community and introduce yourself.

Look for younger people in your classes, jobs, extracurriculars,
or other activities to befriend and pour into.

Write down several questions you'd like to ask a woman who is older than you
and invite her to coffee. Offer to buy the coffee and ask her the questions.

SHARPENED

How God Uses Accountability in Friendship

Kolby Knull

I was fifteen the first time I was confronted with a friend's sexual sin. I found out she and her boyfriend were having sex. I was confused. We were both Christians who believed sex should be saved for marriage. We had always said we were *both* waiting and planned to hold one another accountable. I was sad because I didn't want my friend to live in sin; I felt lost because I had no idea what to do.

When I tried approaching her, I left her feeling judged and shamed. She stopped telling me the details of her life, she began hanging out with girls who were also having sex, and we grew apart. Was I wrong to tell her the truth about what the Bible says about sex? Should I have kept quiet and allowed her to continue engaging in sin?

CHRISTIANS ARE CALLED TO HOLD ONE ANOTHER ACCOUNTABLE.

Read Luke 17:1-5
and then check out the verse below.

Iron sharpens iron, and one person sharpens another.
—Proverbs 27:17

Christians are called to hold one another accountable.

Accountability is meant to help us walk in obedience, stirring us to become more like Jesus. It is like a train that gets us to the destination of sanctification. When we hold one another accountable, we sharpen each other spiritually through reminders of what living a life like Jesus looks like practically.

When I approached my friend, I was more concerned with confronting her sin than with her looking like Jesus. I confused accountability with judgment. Judgment says, "You're a sinner and deserve God's wrath." Accountability says, "We are both sinners and need a Savior."

When we hold one another accountable, we remind each other that God has given us the power to turn away from our sin and toward God. But it can be hard to see the difference between the two. When we can't figure out how to avoid judgment, we may choose to shy away from accountability. But what if we could have friendships filled with grace *and accountability*?

Luke 17:3-5 is a roadmap to what godly, graceful accountability looks like:

LOVINGLY REBUKE: When we call one another out of sin, we do so in gentleness, kindness, and love. A godly rebuke exposes sin with love and points a friend to Christ. An ungodly rebuke brings judgment. How do we know whether we are rebuking in love or judgment? First, ask God to expose the motives of your heart.

Are you more concerned with being right than you are with your friend's heart? Is your goal repentance or shame (2 Corinthians 7:9)?

CALL TO REPENTANCE: Genuine repentance is a heart posture that says, "I will look to Christ for what I thought could be found elsewhere." When we call one another to repentance, it is important to come with humility and honesty. Acknowledge your sin and your need for accountability and prepare by reading God's Word beforehand. Then ask for permission to read the Bible together and uncover what God says about the specific sins.

FORGIVE: To forgive means to overlook an offense and to stop holding that offense over a person. Luke 17:4 says that even if someone repents of the same sin seven times in the same day, forgive them! It can be frustrating, and even heartbreaking, to watch friends sin over and over. But oh, we can show the love of Christ by receiving them back in love!

REPEAT: The person being rebuked in Luke 17 comes back again and again, repenting to the one who rebuked him. Why? Because there is trust when everything is said in love. Although one person kept stumbling, they both knew their friendship was founded on helping one another look like Christ.

LET'S CHAT

Years later, when I was twenty-three, another friend confessed she and her boyfriend were falling into sexual temptation. I was still sad, but this time I wasn't lost! I approached it from a place of *godly* rebuke. I lovingly addressed her sin and

We can show the love of Christ by receiving them back in love!

called her to repent. I chose forgiveness because Christ already forgave her, and I would have done it over and over again if that's what it took. Why? Because Christ forgives me day after day for my sin. I asked her questions, tried to understand what got her there, and leaned on Scripture to help me confront sin *with grace*.

This friend was thankful that I loved her enough to share the truth with her, and it caused her to turn away from her sin and walk in obedience to Jesus.

We *all* sin. When we do, we can confess it to one another, lean on each other, and help point each other back to Christ. *Iron sharpens iron.* As we point one another back to Jesus, whether it's one or one hundred times, we can remind friends that living like Him is better.

Friendships where you do whatever you want, ignore accountability, and demand your way are easy to come by. But godly friendships bring sharpening, growth, transformation, and freedom to be loved fully by those around us.

> We can remind
> friends that
> living like Jesus
> is better.

WHAT ABOUT YOU?

How has accountability with friends helped you and taught you about Christ?

Are there areas of your life where you could use accountability? What are those areas?

In which friendships could you create a culture of accountability? How would you start?

JOURNAL YOUR PRAYERS

Thank God for the gift of accountability and for giving us friends who will walk with us as we struggle to fight sin.

Confess if you have judged friends who are working through sin while ignoring your own sin. Ask God to help you see and address your sin before calling friends out.

_Ask God to bring to you three or four friends with whom to create
an accountability group and to bless your friendships as you pursue
holiness together._

TAKE IT FURTHER TODAY

Start an accountability group and spend time together regularly, confessing sins to one another. Don't be afraid to go first!

Find Scriptures addressing those specific sins and then pray for one another aloud.

Rejoice together in Christ's forgiveness and love for you and be patient with one another as the Spirit sanctifies you all.

LIKE A SURGEON,
FRIENDS CUT YOU
IN ORDER
TO HEAL YOU.

—Timothy Keller

WALKING AWAY

When Friendship Leads to Sin

Cambria Joy

"**S**he doesn't have an eating disorder; she's just trying to be a better dancer. You don't have anything to worry about!"

This is what I'd say to people who were concerned about me and my best friend.

Years after moving to a new town, I *finally* made a friend. It felt like a miracle to have found her. We got along great on the surface, but underneath the hood of our friendship, things were getting dark. My friend was obsessed with her appearance. She was a competitive dancer and told me she needed to be lighter for her flips so that she could score higher in competitions. I was naïve and didn't realize it wasn't normal for her to not eat all morning, drink a small shake for lunch, and pop a laxative after dinner.

To me, she was just trying to be a better dancer. I didn't care what she looked like or how much she weighed. But eventually, her subtle comments weren't just about *her* body—they were about mine too. I didn't realize what was happening until it was too late. She started to control my eating habits at her house and made us start intensely working out. Her comments about my body became more pointed, and for the first time in my life, I looked in the mirror and *noticed* my body—and not in a good way. Deep down I knew I had to walk away from the friendship, but she was my only friend.

How was I going to do it? Could I?

Read Matthew 16:21-28
and 1 Peter 2:11-17
and then check out the verse below.

Whoever walks with the wise becomes wise, but the companion of fools will suffer harm.—Proverbs 13:20 ESV

When friends lead us to sin, it's time to walk away.

The book of Proverbs tells us that we become like who we walk with. We guard our character by being watchful of our company. Who we spend time with will influence not just where we go, but how our hearts are shaped along the way. The people we are closest to have the greatest influence.

Paul echoes this reminder in Corinthians: "Do not be deceived: 'Bad company ruins good morals'" (1 Corinthians 15:33 ESV).

My friend idolized her appearance above everything else. The mirror became something she worshipped, and she and I both suffered a lot of harm because of it. When we fear the Lord, we don't let any other loves take the top spot in our heart. My friend and I didn't fear the Lord—we feared the mirror.

WHEN FRIENDS LEAD US TO SIN, IT'S TIME TO WALK AWAY.

My friend had already let the worship of body image take her down a road I didn't want to travel, but because I was her friend, I ultimately fell down that slippery slope too.

Friends can sharpen us and strengthen us (Proverbs 27:17). They can make us reflect God's image more clearly. But friendships fail to fulfill their purpose when they do the opposite.

LET'S CHAT

Jesus told Peter that when a friendship becomes more focused on the world than it does God, it makes us vulnerable to Satan's attacks (Matthew 16:23). When we're vulnerable, we forget that Satan wants us to walk far away from God and to live a life marked by sin. If Satan can use a friend and all the fun they offer us to lure us away from God, he will. First Peter 2:11 says, "Beloved, I urge you as sojourners and exiles to abstain from the passions of the flesh, which wage war against your soul" (ESV).

I wish my dear friend would have never bought into the lie that a perfect body could make her happy. That lie waged a direct war against her soul. And ultimately, it warred on mine.

We become like the people we walk with. May this be a reminder to walk closest to Jesus, even when it means walking away from certain friends.

Friends can make us reflect God's image more clearly.

Seek friendships that don't lead you down a path of sin, but up a path of seeking Jesus.

Looking into my friend's eyes and telling her I could no longer continue our friendship was one of the hardest things I've ever had to do. But I'm so glad that my fear of God helped me turn back toward Jesus. Fear the Lord, my friend, and seek friendships that don't lead you down a path of sin, but up a path of seeking Jesus.

How might letting a friendship go create more room for a healthy friendship with God?

Have you ever had to walk away from a friendship? Describe that friendship and how God helped you.

How does knowing that God uses other people to shape our character change the way you view friendship?

JOURNAL YOUR PRAYERS

Thank God that He uses your friends to make you more like Him.

_____

_____

_____

_____

_____

_____

_____

_____

_____

_____

Ask God to bring you friends who will help you walk in the way of wisdom.

_____

_____

_____

_____

Confess your need for God to help you not walk in the way of sin in friendships, no matter how fun they temporarily might be.

TAKE IT FURTHER TODAY

Notice when a friend starts to prioritize anything over God.
Watch their words and actions and pray for discernment for how to
speak the truth in love and for when to walk away.

Read your Bible to place truth in your heart. Hide God's Word in your heart,
and it will be a light to your friendships (Psalm 119:105).

Call out sin in your friendships. If you have a friend who is behaving
in a way that values sin over God's Word, consider those things to be red
flags. Be on guard against sin, even if it's not your own.

MARKED BY LOVE

Imitating Jesus in Friendship

I grew up in the concrete jungle that is Dallas, Texas—the city best known for its streak of 110-degree July days.

Reality check: Texas heat exists year-round. And unfortunately for me, I was part of a track-and-field-loving family. Running track (even in Texas) wasn't optional.

Some of my most memorable moments were spent sprinting 200-meter dashes on a red, rubber track in 100-degree weather . . . in *April*. My coaches were the only thing that made those long practices bearable. And all my favorite coaches had one thing in common: they got dirty with me.

The best coaches dripped sweat *beside* me. They demonstrated the drills beforehand. They didn't yell from the sidelines because they were running right next to me. Whatever problem I had, we had it together. Whatever heat we endured, we endured it together.

Their love didn't end with their words; rather, their love led to action.

Read 1 Corinthians 13
and then check out the verses below.

"My children, I will be with you only a little longer. You will look for me, and just as I told the Jews, so I will tell you now: Where I am going, you cannot come. A new command I give you: Love one another. As I have loved you, so you must love one another."
—John 13:33–34 NIV

Godly friendship is marked by love.

You may be familiar with 1 Corinthians 13. This passage is often used to talk about romantic love. However, it is a command for Christians to love one another in every context. The passage is filled with directions on what it means to walk in the way of love.

Verses 4 through 7 define love for us. Love is patient and kind. It does not envy or boast. It is not rude or selfish. Love pursues justice and truth. Love bears the burdens of others. It believes and hopes on behalf of others. And love endures. It lasts forever. In a world that complicates love, the Bible explains it simply.

GODLY FRIENDSHIP IS MARKED BY LOVE.

Every single verse in 1 Corinthians 13 reminds us of Jesus. The words in John 13 were the very words of Jesus at His last meal with His disciples—the disciples He had walked up close with for three years. The best part? The words weren't just *words*. For thirty-three years Jesus demonstrated love through His *actions*.

He was the perfect friend, and He gave us the perfect example of what love in friendship looks like. Jesus is King of the universe, but His love is humble. Philippians 2:6 says Jesus didn't hold His equality with God over the heads of His friends. Instead, the God of heaven and earth humbled Himself.

Jesus never sinned, yet He washed dirty feet. Jesus stepped down from His throne to walk on dusty ground. He dined with the homeless and the weak. He broke bread with tax collectors and prostitutes. He drank water from muddy wells and conversed with the lost. And then, He died a horrific death to save even the "strongest" of us. Jesus got in the dirt with us in every sense of the word. His love led and still leads to action.

True friendship is marked by love. And where love is absent, friendship cannot exist.

LET'S CHAT

I can only imagine how Jesus's love impacted each of the disciples, but I know exactly how His love has impacted me. The best part of the Christian faith is that it doesn't end with Him. When Jesus died on the cross, He defeated death—the death that we sinners should have received.

Love is marked by humility and a tender heart.

He was the perfect friend, and He gave us the perfect example of what love in friendship looks like.

Ephesians 5:1–2 says that because of the sacrifice Jesus made for us, we now get to be *imitators* of Christ. Because of Jesus, we can know how to walk in the way of love with one another. He got in the dirt with us, empowering us to get in the dirt with others!

We live in a world that says love is conditional. The world says, "If it doesn't serve me, it's not for me." Worldly love is transactional and shallow, and it has complicated the way we view friendship.

But I'm here to tell you that loving our friends is simple. The answer to friendship isn't hidden. The key to friendship is written in the Bible. Love is unconditional. Love is truthful and others-focused. Love is marked by humility and a tender heart.

If you want to be a friend, learn the way of love. And if you want to learn the way of love, look at Jesus.

WHAT ABOUT YOU?

What do you think "getting in the dirt" with friends looks like? When was the last time you got in the dirt with your friends?

How do your friendships make you feel?

What are some specific ways you can better love your friends?

JOURNAL YOUR PRAYERS

Thank God for loving you first. Praise Him for being a God who leads by example.

Ask God how you can better love your friends. Pray that He will give you friendships marked by love.

Confess any feelings toward your friends that are not rooted in love.

TAKE IT FURTHER TODAY

Ask your friends how you can pray for them. Set aside a specific
time each week to pray for your friends by name.

Speak to your friends with grace and truth. Text some
encouragement to a few friends today.

Offer to help a friend with school or work in an area
she has told you she's struggling with.

ALL THE WAY
Complete Forgiveness in Hard Friendships

Tara Sun

I was driving home from Costco one sunny day when seven words from a podcast hit me like a sucker punch to the gut: "But have you forgiven *all the way*?" Forgiveness? I wasn't even slightly interested in hearing that word.

A few months after my husband and I got married, one of our best friends cut us out of his life. He had been a friend since high school and stood next to us on our wedding day. His disappearance was out of the blue, and he didn't give us a reason why. We were shocked, to say the least.

How do you forgive someone after that? Time may have been able to mask some things, but it certainly didn't heal this deep ache in my soul. When our friend's betrayal sprang to my mind, all I felt was anger, resentment, and bitterness.

Conviction cut deep as the Lord revealed that I needed to forgive my friend. That podcast blasting through my speakers was like a big neon sign from God, saying, "You haven't forgiven *all the way*."

Read John 13:31-38; 18:15-17, 25-27; and 21:15-19 and then check out the verse below.

When they had finished breakfast, Jesus said to Simon Peter, "Simon, son of John, do you love me more than these?" He said to him, "Yes, Lord; you know that I love you." He said to him, "Feed my lambs."—John 21:15 ESV

Forgiven people forgive people.

In the final chapters of John's Gospel, we read about a handful of interactions between Jesus and His disciples. John 21 tells of a time when Jesus stopped to sit and talk with Peter. Peter was Jesus's disciple and friend, but he had denied knowing Jesus a few days earlier.

Flip back a few pages to John 18. You'll find Peter's unfortunate misstep: his infamous denial of Jesus—not just once but *three* times.

Peter's best friend and Savior was about to be nailed to a cross to die a painful death. Perhaps Peter feared a similar fate. How it must have grieved Jesus to see His friend cave to peer pressure and deny Him in such a public way. How it must have hurt His heart to be betrayed—by not only a friend but also someone who was like a brother.

FORGIVEN PEOPLE FORGIVE PEOPLE.

In John 21, Jesus intentionally, mercifully, and lovingly reunites with Peter. Jesus asked Peter three times if he loved Him. It was the same number of times that Peter had denied Jesus. Our Savior laid aside His pride and hurt to restore their relationship. He had *already* forgiven Peter all the way.

What happened next is just as inspiring, if not shocking:

"Feed my sheep," Jesus said (v. 17).

"Follow Me," Jesus said (v. 19).

Not only did Jesus forgive Peter, but He also invited Peter back into friendship. How easy would it have been for Jesus to forgive Peter but then keep him at arm's length? Wouldn't we say Jesus was justified in not wanting anything to do with Peter? While some friendships do warrant boundaries, caution, and space, Jesus demonstrated the purest kind of forgiveness: holding nothing against Peter from the past, restoring their relationship in the present, and walking life's roads with him in the future.

LET'S CHAT

Forgiveness is not popular. It's not the most traveled road, nor is it praised by the world. The world praises empowering yourself at all costs and putting yourself first. It encourages us to "get even," ruin someone's reputation by gossiping about them, or cut people out of our lives. My friend, Jesus calls us to live by a different set of beliefs—to inhabit His upside-down kingdom, where things may not make sense to the world.

We can forgive all the way, even when it's not reciprocated.

Forgiveness means letting go of lists of how someone has wronged you. It means rooting out bitterness, anger, and resentment in your heart. It means not letting hurt fester. It sometimes means overlooking offense and becoming a kind and honest communicator and initiator when conflict happens in the future.

I know forgiveness isn't a one-way street. Sometimes the other person isn't ready or willing to receive forgiveness.

As I write this, I still have not heard from the friend who cut me out of his life. What do I do with that?

In Romans 12:18, Paul tells us to live in peace with one another, *as far as it depends on us*. We're to do what we can to restore relationships all the way, but we can't make other people pursue peace with us if they don't want to. Sometimes all we can do is forgive from our end and then leave the relationship in God's hands. Get on your knees in prayer and surrender the outcome to God.

The good news is that we can forgive all the way, even when it's not reciprocated.

After all, haven't we been forgiven too? Romans 3:23 says we've all sinned and fallen short of the glory of God. God poured out His forgiveness, and it is not something we are entitled to or deserve. We deserve God's wrath—separation from Him, a severed relationship, and the cutting of all ties to His good gifts.

But God, in His intentionality, love, and mercy, forgave us. Because He did it for us, it's our turn to do it for others.

Forgiven people forgive people. All the way.

Forgiveness is not popular. It's not the most traveled road, nor is it praised by the world.

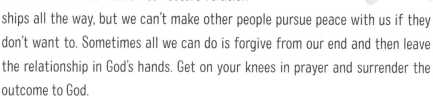

WHAT ABOUT YOU?

Have you ever thought you'd forgiven someone, but then felt bitterness, anger, or resentment creep back in? How did or do you respond to those feelings?

_____

_____

_____

_____

_____

Who in your life have you been withholding forgiveness from?

_____

_____

_____

Make a list of everything you can think of that Jesus went through so you could be forgiven. How does this make you feel?

_____

_____

_____

_____

_____

_____

JOURNAL YOUR PRAYERS

Thank God that He forgave you on the cross and holds nothing against you.

_____

_____

_____

_____

_____

_____

_____

_____

_____

Ask God to help you forgive those you haven't forgiven all the way and pray for opportunities to restore a lost friendship.

_____

_____

_____

_____

_____

Confess any resentment, anger, and bitterness you are harboring against someone. Ask God to show you how to pursue peace in that friendship again.

TAKE IT FURTHER TODAY

Go to your Bible's concordance and look up the word "forgive."
Meditate on a few of those Scriptures each night before you go to bed.

If it's possible or appropriate, set up a time to meet with a friend
who has wronged you. Be willing to say you're sorry for any
wrongdoing and to ask for forgiveness too.

Find a forgiveness accountability partner—someone who knows when
you struggle to forgive and will encourage you. Commit to praying
for one another and checking on each other.

JESUS COMMUNITY

Making Friends Who Take Us to Jesus

I'm a runner.

But not like a track runner. (I consider that the worst form of torture.) *I'm always on the move.*

Always moving toward the next opportunity.

Always moving toward the action.

I love a calendar full of things to do. I love the hustle and bustle of life. I'm like a human city: sometimes sleeping, sometimes extremely noisy, and often chaotic.

So you can imagine my amazement when the coronavirus decided to disrupt all my running. The girl moving one hundred miles per hour had the brakes pulled on her. I found myself free-falling into a quiet, still abyss.

And let me tell you, I was sad. I mourned the opportunities I would miss. I grieved the socializing that would no longer happen. I was devastated about missing out on things I believed God had called me to.

For so long, I was running, doing, going. Suddenly, I found myself spiraling, struggling, stuck. I was unable to move on my own.

I wondered, *How can I get out of this rut? Will I ever get out of it? Is there anyone who can help me?*

Read John 11:1-44
and then check out the verse below.

He heals the brokenhearted and bandages their wounds.
—Psalm 147:3

Real friends take you to Jesus for healing.

Jesus's friend Lazarus was sick, and Lazarus's sisters, Mary and Martha, knew Jesus was the only one who could heal their brother. Lazarus was so sick that he couldn't go anywhere, so they summoned Jesus to take a long trip to come help.

They did not doubt that He could heal their brother.

They knew Jesus loved Lazarus enough to work a miracle.

Lazarus was stuck in his situation physically. There wasn't much he could do to get himself out. He couldn't take himself to be healed; his sickness would soon land him in death's lap. His sisters decided they would make a big, faithful ask of the One who *could* heal their brother: Jesus. They knew that no sickness was too great to be healed by Jesus. They had faith to make big asks of their Savior on behalf of their brother.

Mary and Martha had no idea what they would

REAL FRIENDS TAKE YOU TO JESUS FOR HEALING.

> Lazarus couldn't take himself to be healed; his sickness would soon land him in death's lap.

experience when they asked Jesus to come. They didn't know He would wait. They didn't know their brother would die. They especially didn't know they would watch Jesus do something much bigger than heal Lazarus from a sickness. All they knew was that their friend Jesus could help.

When we are stuck in sin, grief, or sickness, we need friends who trust Jesus the same way Lazarus's sisters did. Real friends point us to Jesus in times of joy and times of sorrow. Real friends love us enough to not only see when we're stuck but also tell us who our healer is.

LET'S CHAT

When I felt stuck, isolated, and lost during the pandemic, I wondered how I would ever get out of my sadness. Praise God, I had incredible friends who knew Jesus was the only one who could heal my heart. They didn't send me self-help platitudes. They didn't tell me how I could numb my pain.

These friends pointed me to Jesus with their words and actions. Whether it was sending me cute mail and packages, having socially distanced picnics, FaceTime calls, Zoom Bible studies, you name it, my friends did it. They repeatedly encouraged me to go to Jesus in gratitude and reminded me of the truth when it was easy to sit in lies. Most importantly, they prayed for me and asked Jesus to comfort me in my sadness. They asked Jesus to enter into my grief and heal my broken heart. Having people who were willing to walk with me and carry me to the One who resurrects life put fresh wind in my sails.

We've all been in a place where we feel emotionally, mentally, or spiritually paralyzed—unable to go to Jesus on our own. Feeling stuck and helpless often leads to isolation, defeat, and shame. But the beauty of community is that real friends not only notice where you are but also love you enough to say, "You can't stay there."

The Bible calls Christians *sisters and brothers*. Our love for one another—especially when we are in need—should look like Mary and Martha's love for Lazarus, their brother.

Maybe your community points you toward people or things other than Jesus. Maybe your community doesn't even notice that you're stuck and need help. God sees you and wants to meet you where you are, help you get on your feet, and walk with you.

My friend, get yourself a community that knows Jesus is your healer. And be willing to remind your people that He intercedes for us, making big, faithful asks of God the Father on behalf of your friends when they are feeling stuck.

A community centered on Jesus knows that the pleasures of earth won't satisfy our deepest needs. A boyfriend, grades, sports, accolades, sex, social media, and money won't fill our need for love, affection, healing, and security. These things can only fully be found in Jesus.

The beauty of community is that real friends not only notice where you are but also love you enough to say, "You can't stay there."

WHAT ABOUT YOU?

Is there an area of your life where your heart feels like it's sick and stuck in bed? What obstacles are in your way of getting to Jesus right now?

Who or what do your friends point you to in your times of need?

How can you better call on Jesus for help when your friends are in need?

JOURNAL YOUR PRAYERS

Thank God for being a healer and restorer. Because of God, all things can be restored. If you find that your heart is hurting, trust that God is near.

_____

_____

_____

_____

_____

_____

_____

_____

_____

_____

Ask the Lord for help to move toward Him. If you know a friend who is stuck in sadness, ask the Lord for wisdom on how to help.

_____

_____

_____

_____

Confess that you try to find help in places and people other than God when you're in need. Ask Him to help you be satisfied in Him.

TAKE IT FURTHER TODAY

If a friend is going through a hard time, do more listening than talking, and then pray that the Spirit will comfort your friend and heal her broken heart.

Study the Bible with your friends. Get to know who God is together.

Memorize Psalm 147 with your friends, and then remind one another of the passage when one of you is going through a season of sadness.

LEARNING TO LAMENT
When It Feels Like God Isn't Providing Friends

Joanne Faith Russell

Before I went to college, I prayed that I would be surrounded by godly friends. I'd never had a solid Christian friend group, and it was something I'd always wanted. I prayed almost every day for friends who would point me to Jesus.

And the answer was *yes*. God sent me an amazing group of friends who pursued Jesus and His holiness during our secular college experience. I avoided plenty of drama, pitfalls, and sin because of those friends, and I was thankful to God because I knew He had provided them.

But college didn't last forever.

After graduation, my friends all moved to various parts of the country, and I moved back home to Nashville. I wasn't close with anyone from high school, and making friends as an adult was hard. I prayed for another solid friend group, but God's answer wasn't *yes* this time.

I was the loneliest I had ever been.

I felt desperate because I had to ask God for help making friends—something other people seemed to do so easily. I wanted friends, I wanted community, and I cried to God constantly. Why was I alone when it seemed like everyone else had an established friend group? Didn't God see me? Didn't He create me for community? Why wasn't He answering my prayers this time around?

Read 2 Timothy 4:9–18
and Lamentations 3 and
then check out the verses below.

Remember my affliction and my homelessness, the wormwood
and the poison. I continually remember them and have become
depressed. Yet I call this to mind, and therefore I have hope:
Because of the Lord's faithful love we do not perish, for his
mercies never end . . . The Lord is good to those who wait for him,
to the person who seeks him.—Lamentations 3:19–22, 25

We can be sad about loneliness while still putting hope in God.

The book of Lamentations was likely written by Jeremiah, who wrote of his sorrow after his city, Jerusalem, was destroyed.

Jeremiah was a great prophet of God, but he was just like any human. He had emotions. When writing Lamentations, Jeremiah was grieving. And in Lamentations 3, his words went back and forth. They both expressed sadness and declared hope in God.

In 2 Timothy 4:9–18, Paul, one of the most faithful Christians in the New Testament, suffered because of his loneliness. He had been deserted by someone who worked closely with him, and his friends had gone to different regions. Yet Paul still trusted God.

We can be sad about loneliness while still putting hope in God.

Like Jeremiah or Paul, you might be grieving the loss of a beautiful season in your life—maybe one that included friendships—and you may feel alone right now. Jeremiah took his feelings—all of them—to God, and Paul was willing to admit his need for community to his friends. Neither man was trying to put on his best face.

In a time of loneliness, Jeremiah knew something profound: though he was sad, God was his portion. All Jeremiah truly needed was God.

People weren't either Jeremiah's or Paul's portion. Better circumstances weren't going to save either of them. Only God could provide everything they needed.

LET'S CHAT

We need community and friends to walk alongside us. But our hope isn't in our friends or even having a great Christian friend group. Our hope is in God, who created friendship and can provide friends for us when we need them most.

Our friends can't always be there when we need to talk, and they don't always have the solution to our problems. But knowing that the Lord alone is enough can help you survive when friendship feels scarce.

It may seem like God is slow to provide friends. But look at Lamentations 3:25: "The Lord is good to those who wait for Him."

Sometimes God answers our prayers quickly. Other times, *it seems like* He is slow to hear our cries. But we can trust that God always gives us what's best for us at the right time. And in the meantime, we can take our sadness to Him.

It's okay to ask God to provide friends for us, but we also must be content if He doesn't answer our prayers the way we think He should.

Real talk: society tells us that our youth is the time to have never-ending fun—that we should have an Instagram-worthy group of friends and that being young should mean we have continual happiness and joy. But that's not always the case. When you feel lonely, or even miserable, it's easy to wonder why, to ask, *Doesn't God see me?* But Scripture tells us that suffering is for our benefit, and it's good to endure it while we're young! (See Lamentations 3:27–28.)

I had multiple relationships in my life that I needed to develop.

God always provides what we need, even if what we need is to lean on Him on our own for a season. And it's okay—even healthy—to tell God we are sad about it.

Eventually, the Lord opened my eyes, and I saw that I did have friends. My friendships just looked different than they did in college. I no longer had a large group of friends, but I had multiple relationships in my life that I needed to develop.

Though it felt like my loneliness lasted forever, the isolation was good for me. I learned who I was apart from my friend group. I had to trust God when things didn't go my way. And I was challenged to wait patiently in hope—not bitterness—because I believe Scripture is true: the Lord is good to those who wait for Him.

WHAT ABOUT YOU?

When do you feel the most alone, and what are some practical steps to remedy those feelings of isolation?

What are some friendships in your life that you need to develop?

What, if anything, have you set as your portion besides God? How can you actively make God your portion during times of loneliness?

JOURNAL YOUR PRAYERS

Thank God for being good to those who wait for Him. Praise Him for being our portion and always meeting our emotional and relational needs.

_____

_____

_____

_____

_____

_____

_____

_____

_____

_____

Confess any time you've looked for things other than God to be your portion. Ask God to help you be satisfied in Him alone.

_____

_____

_____

_____

Acknowledge times you've been impatient for the Lord to act. Ask God to help you wait patiently for Him to provide the right friends at the right times in your life.

TAKE IT FURTHER TODAY

Take your sadness to the Lord by journaling your prayers in a lament journal.

Keep perspective on the positive things in your life by also keeping a praise journal. Write down all the good things God is doing.

Memorize Romans 15:13 to remember your hope in Jesus.

I can no longer condemn or hate a brother for whom I pray, no matter how much trouble he causes me.

—Dietrich Bonhoeffer

ROOT AND FRUIT

Navigating Envy in Friendship

Kathy Krell

I thought envy was my issue.

I constantly wanted what my friends had:

Parents who were still married . . .

Clothes I couldn't afford . . .

A boyfriend . . .

The list goes on.

My heart grew bitter because I thought I deserved what they had more than they did. For a long time, I told myself, *Just stop being envious*. It never worked. I memorized all the right Scriptures too:

Love is patient, love is kind. Love does not envy . . . (1 Corinthians 13:4)

A heart at peace gives life to the body, but envy rots the bones. (Proverbs 14:30 NIV)

For where jealousy and selfish ambition exist, there will be disorder. (James 3:16 ESV)

I even confessed to my small group that I was struggling with envy. I thought my struggle would go away as I got older, but it didn't. It got worse. Why couldn't I turn my envy off? Why couldn't I be happy for others?

Read 1 Samuel 1:1-19 and then check out the verse below.

But the Lord said to him, "Now you Pharisees clean the outside of the cup and dish, but inside you are full of greed and evil."
—Luke 11:39

Envy is never the root of our problems; it is the fruit of a deeper one.

It's easy to look at what we are doing wrong on the outside and simply fix our behavior instead of asking what is going on inside our hearts. Jesus called the Pharisees out for doing that in Luke 11:39. He said they were so focused on outward behavior that they ignored the problem in their hearts.

The Pharisees weren't the only ones who had problems rooted deep within their hearts. In 1 Samuel, a man named Elkanah had two wives, Hannah and Peninnah. The Lord kept Hannah from being able to have children (the Bible doesn't tell us why), but Peninnah had many sons and daughters (1 Samuel 1:4-6).

Peninnah had the one thing Hannah longed for: children. And Hannah had what Peninnah longed for—love from her husband. Year after year, Peninnah cruelly mocked Hannah for being unable to have children.

First Samuel doesn't say how often envy knocked at the door of Hannah's heart or if she grew bitter toward Peninnah. Because Hannah was human, she must have been tempted to be envious. Instead of giving in to temptation and letting her actions be overtaken by

Envy is never the root of our problems; it is the fruit of a deeper one.

envy, Hannah did something else: she prayed. Hannah went into the temple and wept bitterly, pouring out her soul's desires to the Lord. Hannah vowed that if the Lord would bless her with a son, she would dedicate him to God. We don't know every word she prayed, but I imagine she left nothing unsaid before her heavenly Father.

After Hannah prayed the Bible says, "She went on her way . . . and her face was no longer downcast." Downcast is another word for deep sadness. So after her prayer, Hannah's sadness seemed to be gone (1 Samuel 1:18 NIV). Notice something important: the Bible does not say Hannah went away and Peninnah never bothered her again. It does not say Hannah's prayers were answered or that she got what she wanted immediately. Yet she got up and went away . . . happy? How? Three things:

1)   Hannah found the root of her sadness and turned to God!

2)   Hannah was honest with God. She was vulnerable and poured her heart out.

3)   Hannah trusted God and His character. She had faith that everything He was doing—even withholding children from her—served a purpose.

LET'S CHAT

As you watch your friends get things you desperately want, know you are not alone. Maybe a friend got into the college you wanted to get into. Maybe she got a new car, and you have your sibling's hand-me-down. Whatever situation may be tempting you today, I know one thing: God sees you. He understands you,

HANNAH DID SOMETHING
ELSE. SHE PRAYED.

God is the giver
of good gifts,
and He wants us
to come to Him
with our heart's
desires.

and He knows the deepest desires of your heart. Hebrews 4:15 says He empathizes with our weaknesses because Jesus was also tempted.

Hannah reveals something important about our struggle through envy. Envy is a symptom of forgetting who *God* is. Hannah's face didn't become downcast only because Peninnah was cruel—though I am sure her sadness was affected by it. If that were the case, her time with God wouldn't have changed anything, because she still went home to Peninnah's mocking. Envy is not something we work out only between friends; it reveals something within *our* hearts that needs addressing.

When we feel like God is withholding good from us, we've forgotten what James 1:17 says: "Every good and perfect gift is from above." God is the giver of good gifts, and He wants us to come to Him with our heart's desires—not fight with one another about them. Hannah chose to trust that God was a *good* God and that His plans for her life were *good* even when she didn't have a baby. She placed her faith and trust in God because of who He is.

What do you want right now that you don't have?

How do you respond when you see others who have what you want?

Which of Hannah's responses to God is most difficult for you (going to God, vulnerability, or trust)? Why?

JOURNAL YOUR PRAYERS

Thank God for all He has given you.

_____

_____

_____

_____

_____

_____

_____

_____

_____

_____

_____

_____

_____

Confess the times you're tempted to be envious. Get specific! What situations in your life are causing you to feel envy?

_____

_____

_____

_____

_____

Pray for the friends you are envious of. Ask God to bless them, soften your heart toward them, and show you ways to bless them. Ask God for a heart of gratitude and repent of any bitterness you feel.

TAKE IT FURTHER TODAY

Pray for contentment when you feel yourself getting envious.

Set aside 30 minutes to pray, thanking God for who He is and what He has given you. Don't be afraid to ask God for the desires of your heart, but don't forget to remember that He gives all good gifts too.

Memorize 1 Timothy 6:6.

WHEN SEASONS FINISH
Grieving the End of a Friendship

Cambria Joy

Friends are either seasons, reasons, or lifetimes. I heard my mother's words in my mind as my heart ripped in half. Someone I thought would be a lifetime friend was only for a season.

After a long time of not having any friends, I met whom I believed to be my friendship soulmate. Our bond was deep, rich, and like sunshine to my soul; our time together was a golden era full of laughter, sleepovers, and road trips. I couldn't help but think that God had created this person just for me. When she left for college, tears streamed down my face as we separated. I drove away from her house, and she drove hundreds of miles away to live in a dorm and make memories with new people.

Soon, I fell in love. I wanted to process my new relationship with my friend, but I stopped hearing from her. The wedding bells rang louder and more often than her calls and texts. Months after I walked down the aisle, I came to terms with the truth that the warmth of our friendship had faded into the cold of winter.

Recognizing the end of our friendship was like making it to the last page of a book I never wanted to end. But this wasn't fiction. There was no crash landing, but she made it clear we'd grown apart. My friend had seemingly disappeared, and it was like my sadness was the only evidence that she was ever my friend in the first place.

A *season.* How I wished it was an endless summer.

Read 1 Samuel 20
and then check out the verse below.

And as soon as the boy had gone, David rose from beside the stone heap and fell on his face to the ground and bowed three times. And they kissed one another and wept with one another, David weeping the most. —1 Samuel 20:41 ESV

The end of any friendship is sad, and it's okay to grieve.

When this moment in 1 Samuel took place, Saul was king of Israel. He was power-hungry, and he had his heart set on killing David. David was God's choice for the next king of Israel, but he wasn't Saul's son. He was the son of Jesse—*not* the logical heir to the throne. Saul and his family would soon be out, and David would be in. This was not your typical pass-down-the-crown situation. This was God's plan. But Saul's pride grew hot, and his heart became engulfed with jealousy toward David. He knew his kingdom's clock was ticking down.

Jonathan was Saul's son and David's best friend. He wasn't jealous that David would take the throne that should have been his. David and Jonathan were such great friends that Scripture says, "Jonathan became one in spirit with David, and he loved [David] as himself" (1 Samuel 18:1 NIV). Their friendship was stronger than family loyalties.

The end of any friendship is sad, and it's okay to grieve.

Can you believe the heartbreak of this moment? David had to leave his closest, dearest friend because that friend's dad was trying to kill him.

It was the end of David and Jonathan's season of friendship, and when a season of friendship comes to an end, it's only natural for it to hurt the heart.

LET'S CHAT

When we read about Jonathan and David's friendship, it's hard not to long for a friendship knit as tightly as theirs. Their love for one another was so thick that you can feel it as you read about their comradery during tragedy. They didn't want their friendship to be a season; they wished there was no last page of their story.

Though their season's end looked different from mine, the desire for lasting friendship is written in all our DNA. The end of a friendship reminds us of the brevity of life and a deeper truth: things don't last like they should. One day, we will experience an eternal relationship with God and His people.

When a relationship ends here, it is a reminder that one day, relationships will never end again.

David and Jonathan's friendship, though it was for a season, points us to a friendship that will last for eternity.

When a season of friendship comes to an end, it's only natural for it to hurt the heart.

> David and Jonathan's friendship points us to a friendship that will last for eternity.

David and Jonathan's love for one another outlasted their separation. After Jonathan died, David wrote a poem about brotherly love and even continued to care for Jonathan's family (2 Samuel 1).

This is a picture of the love God has for us. It's a permanent, trustworthy promise that God will be faithful to people even when we are not faithful to Him. Walk with Jesus, become His friend, and enjoy the friendship that will truly last forever.

After months of silence from my best friend, a package arrived at my door. It was a late birthday gift filled with thoughtful gifts and a handwritten, heartfelt *sorry* letter. I was relieved, but I knew that things would never be the same. I was heartbroken, but I knew this sadness wouldn't last forever.

We will grieve the end of friendships here on earth. It's okay to be saddened by brokenness. Meanwhile, we can dance in the endless summer that is friendship with God.

WHAT ABOUT YOU?

Have you ever had to grieve the loss of a friendship? How has God used the loss to shape your view of Him?

_____

_____

_____

_____

_____

How can you invite God to help you process through grief rather than suppress it?

_____

_____

_____

_____

How does knowing that God wants to give you the gift of friendship—with the greatest and deepest friendship of Him—change how you view this season of your life?

_____

_____

_____

_____

JOURNAL YOUR PRAYERS

Thank God that He is near to our broken hearts when we grieve.
Praise Him for being near to you.

Ask God to bring you into a lifetime of friendship with Him.
Remember that He is faithful even when we are faithless.

Confess your desire for control over certain circumstances and friendships. Surrender all your friendships to God and trust that He works all things together for the good of those who love Him (Romans 8:28).

TAKE IT FURTHER TODAY

Write down a prayer inviting God into your pain.
Ask Him to heal your broken heart.

Memorize John 15:15 to remember that Jesus is the greatest friend.
Even when other friendships end, His friendship never will.

Express your grief rather than suppressing it. Journal your prayers
or maybe turn up your worship music and sing to God. Let your
emotions spill out, because they're not meant to be locked away.

REFINED BY FIRE

How Hard Friendships Refine Our Faith

Alexis Lee

When I was five years old, I met a girl who would be my best friend for the next fifteen years. We lived lots of life together and shared joy, laughter, cries, hardships, pain, and late-night drives. We spent hours dreaming of raising our kids to be best friends, just like us. Our friendship was perfect.

Until it wasn't.

As we grew older, we disagreed about everything we believed in, and our values slowly drifted apart. Our lives were being shaped in different directions, and our priorities changed. Before we knew it, we were on the verge of a full-blown friendship breakup. But I didn't want a breakup. I wanted to fix it, and I thought I knew just what to say to make it happen.

Have you ever tried to say a tongue twister? Most of the time, the words don't come out the way we want them to. That's how it felt when I was trying to make things right with my friend. Instead of fixing our friendship, I said hurtful things.

When I recognized my mistake, I tried to ask for her forgiveness, but she had no interest. She was the person I trusted with all my secrets and cherished memories, and suddenly, our friendship was over.

Read James 1:1-18
and then check out the verses below.

You rejoice in this, even though now for a short time, if necessary, you suffer grief in various trials so that the proven character of your faith—more valuable than gold which, though perishable, is refined by fire—may result in praise, glory, and honor at the revelation of Jesus Christ.—1 Peter 1:6-7

God can use anything to refine our faith—even difficulty in friendship.

Peter and James wrote their letters to fellow Christians, encouraging them to persevere despite the challenges they were facing. They repeatedly reminded the Christians that this world was not their home. Their citizenship was in heaven. All believers can endure difficult things knowing God is working.

GOD CAN USE ANYTHING TO REFINE OUR FAITH—EVEN DIFFICULTY IN FRIENDSHIP.

GOD CAN AND WILL USE HARD FRIENDSHIPS TO PURIFY YOU.

However, the hardships early Christians experienced were intense. They weren't only having friendship breakups—many of them were being shunned by their family and friends because they chose to follow Jesus. They were being chased down and sometimes killed because of their faith.

James and Peter reminded their readers—and us—that there can be joy in the trials we face because God is faithful to see things through. In any hardship, including fiery friendships, we can *rejoice* because God is using it to strengthen our faith. In every circumstance, we are not defined by our trials. We are *refined* by them.

LET'S CHAT

Did you know that gold, on its own, has impurities in it? But when gold is heated by fire, those impurities start to fall away, and the gold *gains* value.

Sometimes God allows us to go through what feels like a fire so that we can be refined. Even if your mistakes are the reason a friendship ends, your identity is not "friendship failure." And when the end of a friendship isn't your choice, God can use it to teach you endurance in hard circumstances. God can and will use hard friendships to purify you, making you more like Jesus.

Finally, in all seasons of suffering, we see the *result* of that endurance when we immerse ourselves in God's Word when friendships get hard or even end. As long as we live in this fallen world, we will have hard friendships. Yet God makes it clear that suffering and even loss can be used for good. They can make us more like Jesus.

God uses friendship hardships from your past, present, and future for good too. God knows exactly what He is doing in your life and the lives of others when your friendships feel like a fire blazing around you and even when you mess up and say the wrong thing. He knows what friends you need to help you mature and grow in your relationship with Him.

I have deep regrets about the end of my fifteen-year friendship. Still, despite the words I wish I could take back, I can rejoice in the fact that through my mistakes, God used this difficulty to refine my faith. He reminded me that in my weakness, His power is made perfect (2 Corinthians 12:9)! He wants to shape me into someone who looks like Jesus.

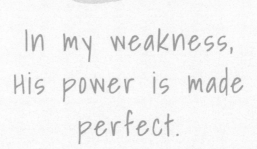

In my weakness,
His power is made
perfect.

WHAT ABOUT YOU?

Have you lost a friend you thought would be in your life forever? How did that make you feel?

_____

_____

_____

_____

What friendships do you need to tend or let go of? How can you pray for that friend?

_____

_____

_____

_____

_____

Which of your friendships have been hard? How can you point to Jesus with that friend?

_____

_____

_____

_____

_____

JOURNAL YOUR PRAYERS

Thank God that despite your inability to be a perfect friend, Jesus made a way for you to have a friendship with Him.

_____

_____

_____

_____

_____

_____

_____

_____

_____

_____

_____

Ask God for His Spirit to work in your heart and to help you be a friend who looks like Jesus.

_____

_____

_____

_____

Confess any bitterness you're holding toward a friend. Ask God to help you forgive and pray for that friend.

TAKE IT FURTHER TODAY

Ask a trusted woman in your life to help you
humbly navigate conflicts in a friendship.

Thank God for your hard friendship. God has
strategically placed you in this friendship for a reason.

If a friend wants to correct or challenge you,
willingly receive their honesty (even if it hurts).

GENERATIONAL FRIENDSHIP

Why Friends Matter Now and Forever

Alma T.

When I was fourteen and my mom was in her late thirties, she passed away of a rare heart condition. It was tragic, and to say that I was heartbroken would be an understatement. I vividly remember the comfort of being surrounded by all my mom's friends from the beginning of those dark, grief-filled days.

When I was in elementary school, my dad traveled often for work. My mom's friend, Nicole, loved my mom so much that she would sleep on the couch, repeatedly, so that my mom wouldn't be scared when my dad was out of town. This was the same friend I sobbed to when I learned my mom died. She's still in my life.

Another one of my mom's friends, Val, was the doctor who broke the news that my mom had gone to be with Jesus. She walked with us tenderly, in a way she could only do because my mom had been a good friend to her.

A few weeks following my mom's passing, I went to camp, and *another* one of my mom's friends made sure I had everything I needed for that week.

The list goes on.

My mom's friendships didn't end with her. They have continued to impact her children—the next generation.

Read 2 Samuel 9 and then check out the verse below.

"Don't be afraid," David said to him, "since I intend to show you kindness for the sake of your father Jonathan. I will restore to you all your grandfather Saul's fields, and you will always eat meals at my table."—2 Samuel 9:7

Your friendships don't end with you.

In the book of 1 Samuel, Saul, king of Israel, grew resentful toward God and hateful toward David after God appointed David as the next king. Saul hated David so much that he attempted to murder David several times! The whole time Saul was trying to kill David, David's best friend was Saul's son, Jonathan.

Despite Saul's wicked plans, God protected David. Fifteen years after David was anointed, Saul and Jonathan were both killed in a battle, and David took the throne as the king of Israel.

YOUR FRIENDSHIPS DON'T END WITH YOU.

In 2 Samuel 9, we learn that though Jonathan had died, David hadn't forgotten him. Jonathan had a son named Mephibosheth. Because Mephibosheth was in Saul's family, he posed a threat to David's throne. In that culture, it would have been customary to kill anyone in Saul's family line to prevent an uprising.

When David realized Jonathan's family was still alive, he recalled their friendship. David thought so highly of Jonathan that he wanted to honor anyone in Jonathan's family. He welcomed Mephibosheth into his home. David chose to not only spare Mephibosheth but also show him kindness.

David and Jonathan's friendship didn't end just because Jonathan died. It went on to bless Mephibosheth—the next generation.

LET'S CHAT

We live in a world of *now*. Everything is easy and fast. With the click of a button, you can have something delivered to your door in minutes. Contracts and opportunities move at the speed of light. We can "make friends" in mere moments, fingers swiping across a screen. It's hard to comprehend that a friendship from my teenage years could have a *lasting* impact.

But I need you to lean in. *Your friendships don't end with you.*

> David and Jonathan's friendship went on to bless the next generation.

Generations will reap the harvest of friendship seeds we sow.

As much as culture may try to fool us into thinking that all that matters is now, our choices have consequences. Something as simple as an act of kindness may have the power to bless people for generations.

As the oldest girl in my family, I was the first to have friends over. My sisters always wanted to hang out with my friends and me. Eventually, I realized they were imitating me. I set their bar for what friendship should look like. My sisters know what kind of friends to look for because of the friendships they've witnessed in my own life.

In the same way I was impacted by friendships that came before me, my friendships impact those who come *after* me! Generations will reap the harvest of friendship seeds we sow. Friendship is a legacy.

Some of my mom's closest friendships began when she was a young woman—even in her teenage years. For many of us, that's *right now*. When we pour into the people around us and allow our communities to pour into us, our friendships will impact generations.

WHAT ABOUT YOU?

How have the friendships of generations before you impacted your life?

What would you like for your generational friendship impact to be?

What does it look like to be intentional about your friendships? How will you ensure that your friendships make a lasting impact on your life and lives to come?

JOURNAL YOUR PRAYERS

Thank God for providing friendships. Praise Him for being a selfless God who cares about the impact of your friendships.

_____

_____

_____

_____

_____

_____

_____

_____

_____

_____

_____

_____

Ask God to teach you how to be a good friend and what it looks like to be intentional in friendship. Pray He will send friends who will have an impact for generations.

_____

_____

_____

_____

Confess any times you haven't valued friendship.

162

TAKE IT FURTHER TODAY

Journal a prayer asking God to use one of your friendships to impact generations. Get specific by using that friend's name. Text or call that friend this week and thank her for a specific way she is special to you.

Do you have a friend who needs something physical? Consider saving your money and purchasing something for that friend who is in need.

Read Luke 1. What do you notice about Mary and Elizabeth's friendship? What qualities of their friendship would you like to be evident in yours?

FIGHTING FOR FRIENDS

How We Help Each Other Walk Away from Sin

Gabrielle McCullough

When you scroll through Instagram and see pictures of what appear to be "godly-girl friendships," you often see a group of girls in fun out-fits at an aesthetic coffee shop with their Bibles open. At least that's what it always *seemed* like to me.

I spent so much of high school looking for picture-perfect friend-ships, but everything changed when I met a friend who showed me what *biblical* friendship looks like. One night, after spending the day hanging out, she called me. With a whole lot of love and truth, she confronted a sinful pattern of pride she saw in me. She told me she had noticed how, in conversations that day, I seemed to find a way to bring everything back to myself. She was *right*. I craved that attention. She pointed me to Philippians 2:3, which says, "Do nothing out of selfish ambition or conceit, but in humility consider others as more important than yourselves."

Though her words were kind, they stung. It was the exact sting I needed.

Read Genesis 14
and then check out the verse below.

Therefore, confess your sins to one another and pray for one another, that you may be healed. The prayer of a righteous person has great power as it is working.—James 5:16 ESV

Sometimes, helping friends get out of sin means walking into dangerous places.

Abram and Lot were family, but they also were business partners and friends. They had traveled together for a long time, but eventually, it came time for them to separate. Lot chose a land he thought would make him rich. He knew the people were sinful and that God would judge them soon (Genesis 13:13), but he chose to go anyway.

Sometimes, helping friends get out of sin means walking into dangerous places.

This choice got Lot into trouble. He allowed his love of money to lead him to a dangerous place. A war broke out in Lot's land, and Lot and his family were in danger. Abram could have looked at Lot's situation and thought, *That's what he gets for choosing riches over obedience to God*. Instead, Abram put everything on the line for Lot. He fought for him! Abram used his wealth to create an army of men to go back and get his nephew, rescuing Lot before his situation got any worse. Abram went to literal war to rescue his nephew Lot from a dangerous and desolate place.

Every single one of us will experience seasons of fighting a war against our sin and the attacks of Satan, our enemy. We will walk through seasons when we are swept away by sin, chasing after the things of this world, and it will lead us into a dangerous place. In those moments, the most loving thing our friends can do is "go to war" for us by calling out our sin and carrying us to the foot of the cross.

LET'S CHAT

Our friends cannot rescue us or heal us from sin. They don't have the authority to forgive our sins, but Jesus does. Our friends' job is simply to help us turn from sin by leading us to the One who has the power to save us.

Abram was willing to run into danger to rescue Lot from the mess he had gotten into. Sometimes when we call our friends out on their sin, it can feel like we are running into a war zone. I am sure my friend felt like that when she called

OUR FRIENDS CANNOT RESCUE US OR HEAL US FROM SIN.

God is so committed to our holiness that He wants to use our every friendship to complete the good work He has started in us.

me out on my pride. She risked the chance of fracturing our friendship. But she loved me so much that she chose to be obedient and to call me out to help me walk away from my sin.

God wants to sanctify you, which means He wants to make you more like Him. One way He does that is through your godly friendships. Even though it might hurt to have a friend confront you, a loving friend will care more about your sanctification (helping you look more like Jesus) than your feelings. God is so committed to our holiness that He wants to use our every friendship to complete the good work He has started in us (Philippians 1:6). When Abraham went into a dangerous place for Lot, and when we go to dangerous places for our friends, we mirror our Savior. Jesus left His throne, came into this broken world, and faced danger like no other to rescue us—the ones He calls His friends.

My friend's words were gracious yet bold. She reminded me of God's Word and the humility Jesus models for us. I thought, *This is what godly friendship ought to look like.* She didn't just want to have fun; she was committed to helping me look more like Jesus.

So let's be girls who look for friends we can pray with and dive into God's Word with. Let's call each other out on our sin, and let's go to war for one another's holiness. Biblical friendship is a tool God uses to make us more holy—more like Him.

WHAT ABOUT YOU?

Do you have friends who call you out and call you toward Jesus? Are you that kind of friend?

How have you pursued sin lately? Which friends can you confess your sin to?

How can you live more authentically with your friends, allowing them to see where you fall short, instead of putting on a mask of perfection?

JOURNAL YOUR PRAYERS

Confess your sin to the Lord and then confess it to a godly friend in your life. Ask that friend to pray for your healing and freedom.

Praise God for His faithfulness and justice to forgive you and purify you. Praise Him for sending His Son Jesus to justify you by His grace.

Ask the Lord to provide friends who will sharpen you and help you follow Jesus. Ask Him to make you that kind of friend as well.

TAKE IT FURTHER TODAY

Be the first to confess sin to your friends
and invite your friends to lovingly correct you.

When you address sin in a friendship, don't shy away
from saying the hard truth, but do it lovingly.

Once you've addressed your friend's sin, hold them
accountable to do the next right thing!

There's no doubt in my mind that what's shaped me and my work more than any particular talent on my part has been living out a calling in the midst of a Christ-centered community.

—Andrew Peterson

A SEAT AT THE TABLE

How to Do Friendship with Unbelievers

When I was sixteen, I was at a party talking to my friend Sarah about church. She looked me in the eyes and asked, "Why would I trust you when you're here doing the same things we are?" I was embarrassed and convicted. She was right. My friends saw me as a hypocrite because no one had helped me understand how to be friends with unbelievers.

As a kid, I was confused about how to do friendship with people who didn't believe in Jesus. I was told to invite unbelieving friends to youth groups and worship nights *but* to be careful about who I spent time with. What was I supposed to do if one of them invited me to a party? Or told me they were sleeping with their boyfriend?

John 17 says that we should be *in* the world but not *of* the world. But how was I supposed to do that?

Read John 4:1–42 and 1 Corinthians 5:9-10 and then check out the verse below.

"The Son of Man has come eating and drinking, and you say, 'Look, a glutton and a drunkard, a friend of tax collectors and sinners!'"
—Luke 7:34

Being a Christian doesn't mean we avoid unbelievers; it changes how we do life with them.

At the start of John 4, Jesus was traveling to Galilee by going through Samaria. At this time in history, most Jews took an alternate route. They avoided going through Samaria because they believed the Samaritans were unclean. Yet Jesus purposefully walked through Samaria, sought out a woman living in sin, and talked to her. (A man speaking to a woman was frowned upon by the Jews.) Jesus addressed her sin and called her to repentance. He promised that what He had to offer was better than her sin. Did He judge her? No. Did He avoid her? No. Did He meet her where she was? Absolutely.

First Corinthians 5:9-10 says it is impossible to avoid unbelievers. Therefore, we cannot and should not try to avoid them! Jesus never avoided unbelievers. He spent time with people who lived in sin, and He never forgot His mission: to show that His love is better than everything else.

Being a Christian doesn't mean we avoid unbelievers; it changes how we do life with them.

When it comes to being friends with unbelievers, we should ask ourselves some questions, ones based on the story of the woman at the well.

AM I WALKING IN GRACE OR JUDGMENT? It's easy for Christians to veer toward one of two extremes: hyper-grace or hyper-judgment.

The person who drifts toward hyper-grace says it's unkind to push your beliefs on people. They avoid speaking the truth to others because they want to be liked. This person forgets the mission of Jesus.

The one who drifts toward hyper-judgment casts shame on others. Like the Pharisees who scoffed at Jesus for eating with tax collectors and sinners, they view others' sins as worse than their own. This person also forgets the mission of Jesus.

Do you see yourself in either description? I fall into both at times. Yet Jesus met the Samaritan woman right where she was. He didn't avoid her because she was in sin, and He didn't affirm her sin. He addressed it and offered her something better: Himself.

WHO IS DOING THE INFLUENCING? In all things, at all times, we are being influenced. To discern whether someone is a good or bad influence, ask yourself if that person is making you more like Christ (Galatians 5:22–23) and the following questions:

- *Are you compromising your morals and falling into sin (1 Corinthians 15:33)?*

- *Can you confidently speak truth to your friends when needed, or are you tempted to hide your beliefs (Ephesians 4:25)?*

JESUS NEVER AVOIDED UNBELIEVERS.

There is no shame in admitting that we sometimes aren't strong enough to resist certain temptations. When others ask why you can't hang out with them when they go to certain parties or listen to specific music, humbly tell them that you want to honor God, but you struggle with temptation in those areas. That's the opposite of hypocritical.

Are we loving our friends like Jesus does? Jesus never avoided unbelievers. He sought them out. He spent time with them (Mark 2:15–16), had compassion for them (Matthew 9:36), and never stopped pointing out their need for Him. Jesus also never shied away from speaking the truth and urging people to repent of their sins. He shows us that to truly love our friends means to speak truth to them. If God is love (1 John 4:16), then genuinely loving others means pointing them to Him! Like this:

> Telling your friends about Christ means doing life with them, living differently, and speaking the truth in love.

- *When friends are heartbroken, tell them He is near the brokenhearted (Psalm 34:18).*

- *When friends feel hopeless, tell them that Christ can be their hope (1 Peter 1:3).*

- *When friends feel unlovable, tell them that Christ loved them enough to die on the cross for them (John 3:16).*

Telling your friends about Christ doesn't mean you're beating a Bible at every moment. It means doing life with them, living differently, and speaking the truth in love so that they get to hear the gospel.

WHAT ABOUT YOU?

Do you find yourself in a hyper-grace or hyper-judgment posture? What makes you think that?

What sins are you wrestling with right now? Are there environments or people that lead you into temptation?

What sins do your unbelieving friends wrestle with, and are there ways you can begin sharing the gospel with them?

JOURNAL YOUR PRAYERS

Thank God for sending Christ to die for you. Praise Him that you get to share your salvation story with others.

Confess if you've been tempted to judge your unbelieving friends or if you have overlooked sin to please them.

Pray for each unbeliever in your life by name and ask God to open their eyes and enlighten their hearts to Him. Ask God to give you the courage to speak truth to your friends, grace for them as they stumble, and wisdom on how to engage.

TAKE IT FURTHER TODAY

Invite your unbelieving friends into environments where you both feel comfortable. Host a girls' night at your house, grab coffee at a cute cafe, or go to a concert or movie.

Get to know this friend by asking questions that make them feel seen.

Don't hide your faith. Tell your friends that you're praying for them, offer to pick them up from a party if they aren't safe, and let them come to you with questions about faith.

Alexis Lee

OUTDOING ONE ANOTHER

Friendship's Effort

Have you ever met someone who makes *everybody* feel like *somebody* and doesn't act like *anybody* else? I am talking about a person who lives differently—someone who carries the fragrance of Jesus (2 Corinthians 2:14).

For the first seventeen years of my life, my faith journey was messy, my friendships did not honor God, and I most definitely did not have the fragrance of Jesus. (My scent was more like the stench of moldy fruit.)

I saw friendship as a way to gain worth and popularity. I wanted to fit in, feel seen, and be known.

Then I met Kati Anne in English class. She was a Christian, and she spent every day of the week answering all my questions about Jesus with patience and love. (I wasn't a Christian yet, so I had *lots* of questions.) She put more effort into our friendship than I had ever experienced before.

She did friendship differently.

I wanted what she had.

I loved the way she loved others and expected nothing in return.

I admired the truth she lived.

I knew what she had was amazing.

Every week Kati Anne sent me Bible verses, helped me study Scripture, and told me how much God loved me even though I wasn't following Him.

Day by day, God changed my heart, and when I started following Him, I no longer wanted to be the type of friend who did everything selfishly. I wanted to self*less*ly love others the way that Jesus loved me.

> ## Read Luke 7:36–50 and then check out the verse below.
>
> *Love one another deeply with brotherly affection. Outdo one another in showing honor.*—Romans 12:10 ESV

Outdoing one another in honor takes effort and sacrifice.

In Romans 12, Paul gives people who are in Christ a brief list of commands for living a selfless life. One of these commands is to love deeply. Though our culture may tell us that love is a feeling, Paul reminds believers to love even when they aren't "feelin' it." Love is a commitment.

OUTDOING ONE ANOTHER IN HONOR TAKES EFFORT AND SACRIFICE.

When I read the story of Jesus and the woman in Luke 7, I am captivated by the woman's effort. She poured out her love before Jesus. She entered a room where she knew she was unwelcome and washed Jesus's feet with her most valuable possession, a bottle of expensive perfume. She sacrificed all these things to show her love for Jesus.

Of course, Jesus is God in the flesh, and our friends are not. But what would it look like to go above and beyond to pour love into our friendships?

- *How can we show more honor to our friends?*

- *How can we make everyone feel like someone?*

- *How can we humble ourselves so that others feel valued, seen, and loved by God?*

LET'S CHAT

The kind of love described in Luke 7 and Romans 12 is a divine love. It exists outside our human capacity. On our own, we love people because it somehow benefits us. A truly selfless-outdoing-in-honor kind of love is nothing we can conjure from deep within ourselves.

What would it look like to go above and beyond to pour love into our friendships?

Challenge yourself to be like the woman in Luke 7, who gave her very best to show love and honor. Consider what you need to give up or what effort you can put in to build strong, lasting friendships.

- Be the first to reach out and make plans.

- Leave notes of encouragement for your friend when you know she is struggling.

- Be quick to listen, slow to speak (even when you want to speak first), and slow to get angry (James 1:19).

- Admit your faults first when you argue and say you're sorry.

- Remind your friends how grateful you are for them!

This is the way my friend Kati Anne did friendship. She daily went out of her way to share the love of God because she was living like Jesus.

My friendship with Kati Anne became one where we could both speak truth into one another's lives. We challenged each other to love like Jesus in our homes, in our schools, and in the world. We outdid one another in showing honor, love, and sacrifice for others to see Jesus.

WHAT ABOUT YOU?

Why was Jesus so honored by the woman who washed His feet? How can you show that kind of honor to a friend?

_____

_____

_____

_____

_____

What friendships are you putting minimal effort into?

_____

_____

_____

_____

_____

How often do you pray for your friends? How can you practically add more prayer for your friends into your daily routines?

_____

_____

_____

_____

_____

JOURNAL YOUR PRAYERS

Thank God that He freely gave us His love without expecting anything in return.

Ask the Lord to provide the strength to love your friends—you can't do it alone!

Confess where you may be seeking your interests instead of ways to serve your friends with sacrificial love.

TAKE IT FURTHER TODAY

Make an index card or sticky note that says, "How can I be the fragrance of Christ in someone's life today?" Place it somewhere you will see it so that you can pray for this opportunity every single day.

Have an assigned day that you talk on the phone, hang out, or catch up with a friend!

Take a friend to coffee and express your gratitude for the way she does a great job of loving you!

Yvonne Faith Russell

WHEN OPINIONS FAIL
A Friend's Words
Are Not Final

A friend's words can sometimes hold more weight than anyone else's. Friends are supposed to speak life. The people closest to you have the biggest influence, and it hurts when their words don't reflect the support and love you thought your friendship had.

Has a friend ever said something to you that you *know* doesn't jive with God's Word? Maybe it's bad advice, like a friend lying to someone about having plans later. Perhaps it's hurtful—a friend telling you that you need to "just get over" the death of a loved one.

Now, our friends can hurl words from behind a screen, and it seems like it's even easier to say hurtful things without much thought. And when we have so many places to get advice from besides the Bible, it's easy for friends to give us platitudes they may have found from a video or heard from an influencer rather than truths from God's Word.

So what happens when we run to a friend for help or encouragement and they say something that's not quite right? What do we do when their words don't line up with God's Word or what His Holy Spirit is saying?

Read Job 42 and then check out the verse below.

After the Lord had finished speaking to Job, he said to Eliphaz the Temanite, "I am angry with you and your two friends, for you have not spoken the truth about me, as my servant Job has."
—Job 42:7

A friend's opinion of you is never greater than God's.

The book of Job tells of when Satan tested a man named Job by destroying his possessions, killing his children, and taking away his health. Job followed God and was righteous before Him, and he tried to make sense of his trials while they were happening. He couldn't understand why he was suffering so much since he had been so faithful to God.

Job turned to his friends for support. Job knew he was right before God, and he wanted to understand why this terrible suffering was happening to him. His friends claimed that no one would suffer like he was unless that person had sinned. They urged him to repent of his sins. They accused him of being unjust to the poor, widows, and those overlooked in society. They said he was secretly wicked and unrighteous.

A friend's opinion of you is never greater than God's.

They believed if Job were truly righteous, or blameless before God, he wouldn't be suffering the way he was. They thought this kind of suffering was strictly reserved for the wicked.

However, Job's friends' opinions didn't align with what Job knew to be true: his relationship with God wasn't the problem.

Job pleaded innocence to his friends and maintained he was righteous. In their attempt to understand Job's suffering, Job's friends mistreated him with harsh words and unfair accusations. They attributed Job's suffering to God's severe judgment.

As those reading this story after it was written, we know how Job's story begins and ends. We can read the first two chapters of Job and see that Satan was acting in Job's life. Though God allowed Job to suffer, God wasn't *causing* the destruction.

Job's friends went on with their accusations for almost the whole book of Job. But in chapter 42, God interjected. God told Job's friends they hadn't spoken the truth about Him. They not only misspoke about Job, but they misrepresented God.

Job's friends couldn't see the whole picture.

LET'S CHAT

Although Job's friends claimed to have wisdom and understanding, they misapplied their "knowledge." They used their understanding, *not* God's wisdom, to explain Job's situation. Although Job trusted his friends, they didn't have the final say about his situation—that was up to God.

Through our knowledge of God and His Word, we know God has told us to do things that don't make sense to everyone else. He instructs us to maintain purity, serve others, and be obedient to God's plan for our lives. But our friends might not be able to see or comprehend why we would do those things.

Similarly, when we hear about our friends' situations, we should be careful not to just say what we think without consulting the Bible first. It's easy to forget that we don't see the big picture. But God does. God knows everything about the past, present, and future, and He's in charge of it all. (See God's reminder in Job 38–41.)

Before advising a friend or taking a friend's advice, go to Scripture.

When we know God's Word, we can filter everything our friends say through it. We can also be friends who go to God's Word *before* giving our opinions and advice.

Our words and our friends' words, no matter how weighty, are not final. Only God's will and words are.

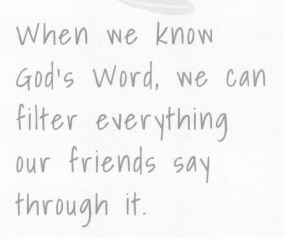

When we know God's Word, we can filter everything our friends say through it.

WHAT ABOUT YOU?

In times of suffering, how do you typically respond?

Who can you go to for help during hard or trying times?

How can you make sure you give encouragement and advice that lines up with God's Word?

JOURNAL YOUR PRAYERS

Praise God for His infinite knowledge and wisdom. Thank Him for providing people who speak the truth about Him into your life.

Thank God for being good in all seasons, even the difficult ones. Ask Him to help you trust Him despite your circumstances.

Confess any judgment you've passed (outwardly or inwardly) when life hasn't gone as planned for someone you know. Ask God to cultivate in you a heart of compassion and understanding for friends going through trying times.

TAKE IT FURTHER TODAY

Listen first and fully before you give advice.

Acknowledge verbally that you can't see the big picture.

When you don't know what to say, go to Scripture
so that you speak only what lines up with God's character.

TOGETHER IN EVERYTHING

Why Friends Should Never Suffer Alone

It was the worst day of my life. There I lay on the cold, hard ground. I felt lonely and isolated. No one could feel my pain—not physically or emotionally. I reached for my phone, called my best friend, Veronica, and choked through tears that I'd had a miscarriage—my tiny baby God was knitting together in my womb had died—and my soul was crushed.

At that moment, I knew exactly what the writer of Psalm 23 meant when he wrote about walking through the valley of the shadow of death. No one wants to walk through the valley of the shadow of death. Especially not alone.

Our conversation was mostly sobs with just enough words from me to explain what had happened. Saltwater tears became our language, and they spoke clearer than any word in the dictionary could have. We spent hours talking on the phone. She carried my grief as it poured out of my heart.

I didn't know what I expected Veronica to say, because what *could* be said? I just wanted my friend. Over that phone call, her presence reminded me that I wasn't alone in this storm. She didn't fix me; she met me in my deepest pain.

When my friend saw me crushed by pain, her immediate posture was knees bent in prayer and a shoulder for me to cry on. She helped me bear the weight of a sadness I couldn't carry alone. She didn't sit back and watch me struggle; she entered the suffering with me, not with words, but with *herself*. She did exactly what a friend is born to do.

Read Matthew 26:1–44
and then check out the verse below.

A friend loves at all times, and a brother is born for a time of adversity.—Proverbs 17:17 NIV

One gift of friendship is not having to walk through suffering alone.

Because every person is born into a broken world, all people will experience suffering. But it's not God's plan for us to suffer alone. He is with us, and He also provides people to walk with us during hardship. Our greatest need in friendship is not only for someone to laugh with us but also for someone who will walk with us on the roads we cannot go alone.

It makes me think of Jesus in the garden, right before He faced the greatest chapter of suffering ever written in history: His death on the cross.

Taking along Peter and the two sons of Zebedee, he began to be sorrowful and troubled. He said to them, "I am deeply grieved to the point of death. Remain here and stay awake with me." (Matthew 26:37–38)

One gift of friendship is not having to walk through suffering alone.

In Jesus's deepest, darkest hour of suffering, as He was about to walk through the valley of the shadow of death, He wanted His friends to *be* there with Him. That was His request. Not a very big ask, but when Jesus came back from praying, He found His friends fast asleep. He woke them up and went to pray again, desiring they stay awake with Him. Coming back again, He found they could not keep their eyes open. His desire for companionship never wavered, even though the disciples did.

Jesus was fully human, and His wish for frienship in suffering proves that none of us are meant to walk through suffering alone. And, even though the disciples failed, just as we all do, take note of this: Jesus reached out to friends when He was drowning in sorrow.

LET'S CHAT

When stormy seas arise in your life, remember God is with you. And if you can, pursue godly friendships before the storms come. Those friends can remind you of God's presence in your life and love you through your sadness.

Will they be there for you perfectly? Maybe not. (Remember, only Jesus is the *perfect* friend.)

Sometimes, we risk getting hurt when we invite people into our suffering. During my miscarriage, I reached out to another family member who did not make me feel loved. She made me feel like my suffering wasn't that big of a deal.

Bringing my friend into my sadness was well worth the risk.

Her response made me feel worse. I asked other friends to pray for me about my frustration with her, and they reminded me that Jesus has forgiven me so much—how could I not extend forgiveness when Jesus didn't withhold it from me?

Look at how Jesus responded when He found His disciples asleep:

> He said to Peter, "Couldn't you stay awake with me for one hour? Stay awake, and pray that you won't be tempted. You want to do what's right, but you're weak." (Matthew 26:40–41 GWT)

In Jesus's deepest, darkest hour of suffering, He wanted His friends to be there with Him.

Jesus expressed how He felt. He didn't withhold the truth. When our friends let us down in seasons of suffering, we can tell them we feel disappointed. Even Jesus's closest friends disappointed Him and let Him down. He knew they would do this, and He invited them into His sadness anyway.

My friend, Veronica, loved me well through one of the hardest seasons of my life. Her presence reminded me that my suffering doesn't need to be experienced alone. Her simple act of opening her ears made me feel loved. Her love reminded me of the love of God. Bringing her into my sadness was well worth the risk.

Next time your heart is carrying something heavy, let someone into your sadness.

Jesus will comfort you through His people. Let Him.

WHAT ABOUT YOU?

Describe a time you have been there for a friend in a difficult time.

How has a friend helped you walk through a trial?

Read Psalm 23. How does knowing that God sometimes comforts us through His people change how you view the "valley of the shadow of death"?

JOURNAL YOUR PRAYERS

Thank God that He always loves us and that His love is more than enough.

_____

_____

_____

_____

_____

_____

_____

_____

_____

_____

_____

_____

Ask God to bring you friends who will walk with you in life's trials and tribulations.

_____

_____

_____

_____

Confess your desire for God to help you in your weakness, to help you be the friend He desires you to be.

TAKE IT FURTHER TODAY

Consider words or phrases that are comforting or
not comforting to you when you're suffering. Text comforting
words to someone you know is suffering today.

If you live near a friend who is suffering, buy her favorite drink
from a coffee shop, take it to her, and offer to be with her.

Don't feel the need to have the right words to say to someone
who is suffering. Your presence will say everything.

AWAY FOR A WHILE

When Friends Should Separate

Alena T.

I am the hardest-core, die-hard loyalist you'll ever meet.

I don't think there is anything sweeter than an elementary-school friendship, and I had just that. I met my best friend in the third grade, and we clicked. She was the friend I'd have long-streak sleepovers with. I would go to her house, and no one knew when I would return to mine (except for my mom, when she arrived to pick me up, reminding me that I had a family at home). We stayed close through middle school.

Then high school happened.

As I changed, so did my friendships. For my best friend and me, there was no giant fight or wild change in opinions or beliefs. We just grew in different directions. And at age seventeen, I let my best friend go. I discovered that sometimes, friends must separate.

Insert dagger into my heart.

Learning that friendships don't always work out is not only confusing; it's also painful. The hardest part, to me, anyway, is that sometimes, friends separating is biblical. Sometimes, it's what God requires.

Read Acts 13:13-15; 15:36-41
and then check out the verses below.

They had such a sharp disagreement that they parted company.
Barnabas took Mark and sailed for Cyprus, but Paul chose Silas
and left, commended by the believers to the grace of the Lord.
—Acts 15:39-40 NIV

For God to be glorified, friends sometimes must separate. And that is okay.

In the book of Acts, the Bible records two Christ-followers—missionaries, actually—*separating.*

In Acts 9, God saved Paul, a known persecutor of Christians. God sent a disciple named Barnabas to encourage and mentor Paul in his early days as a Christian.

When Paul and Barnabas went on their first missionary journey, they traveled with several companions, including John Mark. In Acts 13:13, Paul and Barnabas set out to sea, but John Mark left them to go home to Jerusalem. The Bible doesn't say why he left, but it's possible John Mark was overwhelmed by the intensity of their missionary journey.

For God to be glorified,
friends sometimes must
separate. And that is okay.

Not much is said following John Mark's departure in the rest of the chapter. But in Acts 15, things take a turn.

Paul and Barnabas completed their first missionary journey, and Paul wanted to return to some of the places they'd visited to see how the Christians were doing. Acts 15:37–38 says, "Barnabas wanted to take John, also called Mark, with them, but Paul did not think it wise to take him, because he had deserted them in Pamphylia and had not continued with them in the work" (NIV).

Paul didn't want to bring John Mark because he had deserted them; Barnabas insisted they bring John Mark anyway. This "sharp disagreement" led to their separation.

The Bible doesn't give many details about their dispute. God's opinion on their separation remains hidden, and it's not clear if either man sinned in the process. What is clear, however, is that Paul's and Barnabas's ministries continued, the church kept growing, and God continued to be glorified. Paul's mission expanded and was fruitful, and Barnabas went on to Cyprus to share the gospel.

LET'S CHAT

I can't help but wonder what would have become of Paul and Barnabas's ministries had they stayed with one another. I wonder if future quarrels and disagreements would have dimmed the light they were trying to spread. Would Paul and *Silas* have been able to do the same work they did after Paul and Barnabas separated?

Paul's and Barnabas's ministries continued, the church kept growing, and God continued to be glorified.

As Christians, God calls us to fight for unity. The word "separation" doesn't scream togetherness. However, I'd like to challenge you with a thought: what if unity doesn't mean 100 percent agreement in all areas but rather full agreement in *the* area that matters most?

Paul and Barnabas still believed Jesus was the Messiah, and both made it their mission to tell the world about Him. Just because they couldn't do it together doesn't mean they weren't unified in Christ. Later in the New Testament, we learn that Paul and Barnabas reconciled.

I'm not asking you to say goodbye to all your friends with whom you have differing opinions. What I *am* asking you to do is to not be surprised when quarrels and disputes arise in even God-honoring friendships. When sin or differences in belief become apparent, widen your lens and think with a *kingdom perspective*—see things from God's point of view. Search your heart for friendships you are holding onto that may be keeping you from growing into who God has created you to be.

Seasons change. Visions change. Running the same race can look a hundred different ways.

My friend and I were running the same race. We were just on different courses. That meant we couldn't be side by side as we ran. You have permission to enter new seasons, even to separate, and you must give your friends permission to do the same. That is true friendship.

And remember—even though we may have to separate from some of our friends for a little while, there will come a day when Jesus makes all things, including broken relationships between Christians, new.

> When sin or differences in belief become apparent, widen your lens and think with a kingdom perspective.

WHAT ABOUT YOU?

How would you define unity? Do you view it any differently after reading this devotion?

_____

_____

_____

_____

_____

Do you trust God with your friendships? Why or why not?

_____

_____

_____

_____

_____

Is there a friendship you need to separate from? How might separation between friends bring God glory?

_____

_____

_____

_____

_____

JOURNAL YOUR PRAYERS

Thank God for being a God of unity. Praise Him for being a God who longs for His people to be unified.

Ask God to reveal the friends you may need to separate from. Pray that He will present you with friends specifically designed for your season of life.

Confess any feelings of bitterness or resentment you hold toward your friends with differing opinions. Acknowledge it is okay to disagree.

TAKE IT FURTHER TODAY

When you need to walk away from a friendship,
ask an older woman you know and trust to pray for you.

Make a list of friends you can invest in after you walk away from a friendship.

When you are walking away from a friendship, confess any sin you need to
and ask for forgiveness if you have wronged that friend.

IF I LOVE GOD,
I MUST LOVE PEOPLE.
I DON'T HAVE THE CHOICE
TO CHOOSE WHEN.

—Jackie Hill Perry

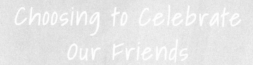

TOSSING CONFETTI

Choosing to Celebrate
Our Friends

Blink.

Blink.

Blink.

No matter how long I stared at the screen, my brain had trouble processing what was on the feed right in front of me.

There it was for me and the rest of the world to see: one of my best friends was smiling from ear to ear, tears in her eyes, and wearing a bright, dazzling engagement ring on her finger.

As I scrolled through the various comments of "Congrats!" and "OMG ILYSM YOU DESERVE THIS," I couldn't help but feel a tinge of sadness. In what should've been a moment of celebration for my friend, I felt envious. As though I lost somehow. As if I were robbed of my dream. As if it slipped away from me before my eyes and landed in her lap—or in this case, around her finger.

It may be seeing one of your best friends get engaged. Maybe it's that a friend got into the college you wanted to go to. Perhaps you have a friend who always gets what they want when you don't. Maybe your friend is getting the attention from an *in* crowd that you secretly desire. Envy creeps into every friendship.

What do you do when the thing you've prayed for happens for someone else? How do you celebrate what God has done in a friend's life without enviously comparing it to your own?

Read Luke 15:11–32 and then check out the verses below.

"His father said to him, 'Look, dear son, you have always stayed by me, and everything I have is yours. We had to celebrate this happy day. For your brother was dead and has come back to life! He was lost, but now he is found!'"—Luke 15:31–32 NLT

Choosing celebration over envy leads to greater joy in friendship.

In Luke 15:11–32, Jesus shared a parable that involved three people: a father and his two sons.

In the culture at that time, all sons were entitled to an inheritance from their father once they hit a certain age. In this family, however, the younger son wanted to collect his inheritance early, essentially wishing his father dead. He was greedy and careless, and after some wild living, he ran out of money. He went back home to his father in shame. Though he deserved to be sent away, his father forgave him and threw a party in his honor. He gathered the whole household to celebrate his son's return!

Choosing celebration over envy leads to greater joy in friendship.

Everyone was ecstatic at this miraculous homecoming—everyone, that is, except one person.

Upon hearing that his younger brother was home, the older brother became envious of and angry about the celebration. Instead of focusing on his brother's heart change and homecoming, he focused on what was missing. He had done all the right things, but *he didn't get a celebration*.

The older son valued the party his dad threw more than he valued his brother. He let envy get the best of him.

Often, we act the same way in our relationship with God. We cherish what God does for us more than God Himself or his children—our spiritual brothers and sisters. God is our provider, but He is so much more than *just* our provider. He is holy, faithful, and forgiving. Out of His kindness and love for us, He gives good gifts.

But when those good gifts go to our friends instead of us, it's hard to not feel envy.

LET'S CHAT

To envy is to believe three lies:
1) Other people seem to have it better than me.
2) I don't have enough.
3) God is keeping things from me.

WE CHERISH WHAT GOD DOES FOR US MORE THAN GOD.

Comparison is not only the thief of joy—it's the catalyst to envy.

Whenever we find ourselves believing these lies, we create narratives that aren't true and miss the opportunity to celebrate God's good gifts for our friends. The reality is, God loves us deeply. Celebrating others doesn't rob us of anything except envy.

In my case, I had to shift my eyes off myself and realize that my friend was receiving a good gift from God! God had heard her prayers for a husband and delivered! And that is good news worthy of celebration! Taking my eyes off myself and putting them on the goodness of my heavenly Father helped me give thanks to God.

My friend was simply the recipient of a gracious gift. Her engagement season was an opportunity to love her well.

Celebrating friends who are where we want to be helps us see God's kindness. Instead of focusing on what we don't have, we can turn our eyes to God, who will not keep anything good from us. He is the giver of *every* good gift. We can throw some confetti on our friends when they receive something worth celebrating. We can rejoice in the fact that God's blessings overflow to our friends and everyone around us!

We can throw some confetti on our friends when they receive something worth celebrating.

WHAT ABOUT YOU?

Who do you compare yourself to? What does this person have that you believe you lack?

What would it look like for you to genuinely celebrate that person?

How does knowing God is the giver of every good gift change how you celebrate others?

JOURNAL YOUR PRAYERS

Thank God for who He is. Reflect on His nature and what makes Him good versus just the good things He does for you.

_____

_____

_____

_____

_____

_____

_____

_____

_____

_____

_____

_____

Ask God to reveal any jealousy, envy, or bitterness in your heart. Is there someone you've distanced yourself from because of this? Ask God for guidance and forgiveness.

_____

_____

_____

Confess to the Lord ways you may have distanced yourself from others. Ask Him for specific people to both privately and publicly celebrate.

TAKE IT FURTHER TODAY

When you begin to feel envious of a friend, immediately pray
and thank God for the good gift He has given to your friend.

Keep a blessing journal and write down five things you've received
or are thankful for every time you compare yourself to a friend.

Regularly tell your friends that you're grateful for
how God is blessing them.

PEACEMAKERS
FOR LIFE

When Friends Need
to Reconcile

I used to think conflict was *bad*—something to be avoided *at all costs*.

When a good friend and I were playing games in a group setting, my friend made several sarcastic jabs at me throughout the night. I was hurt and felt insecure. Eventually, my feelings led to anger—I didn't want to forgive her. But I didn't want my friend to think I was sensitive and couldn't handle a few sarcastic comments either, so I allowed time to go on without addressing my hurt. I avoided conflict and called it peacemaking.

But by avoiding conflict, I wasn't a peacemaker. I was a peace*faker*. I was excusing sin and trying to act like everything was okay, even when it wasn't. I thought that if I addressed the hurt, it would only make things awkward and worse than they already were.

God invites us to view conflict in a different way: to view it as an opportunity to glorify God, encourage one another, and unify us more.

Gabrielle McCullough

Read Genesis 50:15–21
and then check out the verses below.

*All this is from God, who through Christ reconciled us to himself
and gave us the ministry of reconciliation; that is, in Christ
God was reconciling the world to himself, not counting their
trespasses against them, and entrusting to us the message of
reconciliation.*—2 Corinthians 5:18-19 ESV

When friends address conflict well, it can bring reconciliation.

In the story of Joseph and his eleven brothers (Genesis 37–50), we see a desperate need for reconciliation. Joseph's brothers were jealous because their father Jacob showed Joseph favoritism. Their jealousy drove them to hatred, and they sold Joseph into slavery.

God was faithful to Joseph, even during his years of slavery and prison. God eventually brought Joseph into a position of power in Egypt. Several years after that, Joseph, his brothers, and their father were reunited. Joseph forgave his brothers and reconciled with them.

But after their father died, Joseph's brothers were afraid that Joseph would seek revenge for all the ways they had hurt him. You might say they wondered if he was just faking peace the whole time. They begged for their brother's forgiveness and reconciliation. They wanted to repair the relationship they had broken.

When friends address conflict well, it can bring reconciliation.

Joseph could have chosen to hold these sins against his brothers forever, but he chose forgiveness and reconciliation. Joseph allowed God to restore these broken relationships, despite how he had been hurt. He said, "You planned evil against me; God planned it for good to bring about the present result—the survival of many people. Therefore don't be afraid. I will take care of you and your children" (Genesis 50:20–21).

Like Joseph's relationship with his brothers, our relationship with God is fractured because of sin (Romans 3:23). But God didn't ignore the conflict between us. He sent Jesus, who lived a perfect life, died on the cross, and rose from the grave to make our relationship with God right again (2 Corinthians 5:18–19).

LET'S CHAT

If God did that for us, shouldn't we do the same for others? We can forgive because God first forgave us (1 John 4:10–11, 19). We don't have to move away from those who have wronged us; rather, we can move toward them. We can be gentle with others because God has been gentle with us.

Maybe the first glimpse you had into conflict was your parents arguing, your sibling getting on your nerves, or a breakup scene on TV. Perhaps you've viewed conflict as something that only tears people apart and always makes things worse.

GOD DIDN'T IGNORE THE CONFLICT BETWEEN US.

It took me a long time to learn that conflict can be healthy. For a while, I was on an endless search to find a friend with whom I never had any conflict. A friend who never failed me and never hurt me. Guess what? That search came up empty *every single time*. The last thing I naturally want to do when someone hurts me is to respond in humility, gentleness, patience, and love. I would rather choose pride, anger, impatience, and revenge.

But then I remember Jesus.

Jesus was hurt and betrayed by His friends. Instead of choosing retaliation, He chose forgiveness. He didn't fake peace by pretending everything was okay; He didn't break peace by abandoning His friends; He made peace with them.

> Instead of choosing retaliation, He chose forgiveness.

Conflict doesn't have to tear friends apart, and it doesn't have to be ignored. God asks us to fight for unity. That means we chase reconciliation and peacemaking—not division, unforgiveness, or peacefaking. This is what reconciliation looks like: we move toward those who have hurt us and choose to forgive them, no strings attached.

We enter friendships thinking, *This friend surely won't ever hurt me*. But that's an unrealistic expectation—they *will*. You will be disappointed if you put that kind of unbearable expectation on a friend. Your friends will hurt you at some point, and you will hurt them. Conflict is inevitable in our relationships because we are sinners, and doing life with others is simply messy at times. When someone hurts you, it's natural to want to run the other way so that they can never hurt you ever again, but this isn't the way of Jesus's followers.

God invites us to pursue reconciliation. We must be ruthlessly committed to being peacemakers. Let's acknowledge a grievance, and let's commit to pursuing forgiveness and reconciliation.

WHAT ABOUT YOU?

Is there any friend you need to be reconciled to? Write a plan for how you will chase reconciliation in that friendship.

Why is it hard to resolve conflict? What makes it awkward or difficult?

How does the forgiveness you have received through Jesus impact the way you treat friends who hurt you?

JOURNAL YOUR PRAYERS

Praise God for the reconciliation you have received through the work of Jesus on the cross.

Ask God to give you a biblical view of conflict so that through conflict, you can glorify Him and build others up.

Pray for your friendships that need reconciliation and ask God to give you wisdom for pursuing unity.

TAKE IT FURTHER TODAY

Read Ezekiel 36:26. Ask God to give you a heart of love and gratitude
toward your friends, especially friends who have hurt you.

Address and apologize for your sin, before focusing on your friend's sin.

Journal your prayers. Ask God for miraculous healing
in any broken friendship!

WOUNDED

Having Friends Who Will Call Out Our Sin (Even if It Hurts)

Alexis Lee

Have you ever exercised so hard that your muscles ached for days? This part of working out never really *feels* good. It's uncomfortable—it may even feel like a wound. When we work a muscle, its tiny strands tear apart. Over the next couple of days, we feel sore as those strands heal and grow even stronger.

Sometimes, this is how accountability in our sin feels. I had been following Jesus for a solid year before I opened up to a trusted friend about my sexual sin. It was my best-kept secret, and I knew it was time to get some accountability.

Accountability was helpful at first, but soon enough, my struggle only seemed to get worse. Not only did I continue to struggle with sexual sin, but I also had no desire to pray, read the Bible, or even talk to God or my friend about it anymore.

One day, my friend came to me and asked me about my sin. She told me she had noticed I was trying to handle that sin on my own. She reminded me I needed to start spending time in prayer and reading the Bible again and stop making room in my life for time to sin. She offered to keep holding me accountable like she had before.

It stung to hear her words. I hated being called out for the things I felt most ashamed of. Though her words felt wounding, they were true, and they were exactly what I needed to hear.

God gave me a friend to tear the strands of my sin apart so that I could grow to be more like Him.

Read Galatians 6:1–10 and Matthew 18:15–20 and then check out the verse below.

The wounds of a friend are trustworthy, but the kisses of an enemy are excessive.—Proverbs 27:6

True friends lovingly show us our sin and call us to repentance.

There are times when we must be called out for our sin. We need friends who will do that for us, and we need to be willing to do it for our friends too.

When a true friend lovingly confronts our sin, it will probably hurt. But praise God that they are willing to be the bad guy for our good! We don't just need friends who will lie to us to make us feel better about ourselves; we need friends who will correct us when we are wrong.

True friends lovingly show us our sin and call us to repentance.

> Holding one another accountable isn't friendship ending, but friendship building.

In the same way, we need to be willing to address our friends' sins when they are wrong. According to Galatians 6:1, "If anyone is caught in any transgression, you who are spiritual should restore him in a spirit of gentleness. Keep watch on yourself, lest you too be tempted" (ESV). We need the Holy Spirit as we encourage others to be more like Jesus. He will help us be gentle and full of forgiveness. We can be compassionate and caring while speaking truth in love.

God plans for friends to show us our sin and remind us to be more like Jesus. It won't always be pretty or "social media worthy." It will feel uncomfortable and wounding. But *this* is the beauty of being a follower of Jesus: holding one another accountable isn't friendship ending, but friendship building.

LET'S CHAT

We can call a friend to be more like Jesus when:

- . . . she is in a relationship that leads her into a cycle of sin.

- . . . she prioritizes looking cool over showing kindness.

- . . . she is caught in a cycle of gossip.

- . . . a sin pattern persists.

We also need friends who will do the same thing for us.

We know that as we push through the discomfort of being honest about our sin, we build strong muscles. The result makes the pain worth enduring.

When we surround ourselves with people who will "wound" us for the sake of making us more like Jesus, we find freedom, community, and a stronger relationship with Christ. We become a team, doing spiritual conditioning together.

- Together, we will be better able to resist sin.

- Together, we will be more likely to pray for one another.

- Together, we will care about each other at a soul level.

True friends lovingly show us our sin and call us to repentance. They call us to look and act more like Jesus. Their correction may hurt for a little while, but it will only lead to the growth of our spiritual muscles!

We become a team, doing spiritual conditioning together.

WHAT ABOUT YOU?

What sin do you need to be called out on to become more like Jesus? Are you willing to acknowledge that sin if a friend confronts you?

_____

_____

_____

_____

_____

What friends in your life need to be faithfully wounded to grow closer to Jesus?

_____

_____

_____

_____

How can you create a healthy environment in your friendships to have open conversations about sin?

_____

_____

_____

_____

_____

JOURNAL YOUR PRAYERS

Thank God that He saved you from your sin and continues to work in your heart.

_____

_____

_____

_____

_____

_____

_____

_____

_____

_____

_____

Ask God if there are areas in your life or in your friendships where you have sinned and need the help of the Holy Spirit to have conversations about those things.

_____

_____

_____

Acknowledge that through the cross you are and can be holy because of what Jesus has done for you.

TAKE IT FURTHER TODAY

Talk with a friend who follows Jesus and wants to help you grow closer to God about any weak spots (sin struggles) in your life.

Pray that God will soften your heart to be open when others call out your sin.

Look for the fruit of the Spirit in people's lives and develop friendships with those whose lives reflect God's Spirit.

SEASONS OF WAITING
Trusting That God Will Provide Friendships

It was the first time I had been in school in over a year.

When I was a freshman, I was diagnosed with fibromyalgia, a chronic illness that confined me to my bed for months. After an excruciating year of therapy, I resumed school, sports, and life as normal.

But as I took my first steps down the halls, anxiety bubbled within me.

It felt like anything *but* normal. Not only had my physical condition changed, but also all my friendships had changed. While I was in hospital beds and therapy rooms, everyone else was making friends, hanging out, and getting to know one another.

I took a deep breath in and breathed it out. My heart beat fast. I ached for friendship. Ached to be seen. Ached to be known. I wondered if I would ever have meaningful friendships at school again.

Read Matthew 6:25-34 and then check out the verses below.

Do not be anxious about anything, but in everything by prayer and supplication with thanksgiving let your requests be made known to God. And the peace of God, which surpasses all understanding, will guard your hearts and your minds in Christ Jesus.
—Philippians 4:6-7 ESV

God is the giver of every good and perfect gift—including friendship.

Philippians is known as the most joyful book in the Bible. The author, the apostle Paul, wrote this letter to the church at Philippi while he was wrongfully imprisoned. Ironic, right? It's hard to imagine that being under arrest would be a time when someone would feel peace, much less joy. Paul wanted to encourage the church to live as citizens of heaven, not of earth—to live with God's greatness in mind, to remember they wouldn't live on earth forever, and to treasure what God treasured instead of the temporary comforts the world had to offer.

Jesus also encouraged His followers to not be anxious about anything (Matthew 6:25-34), because He cared for them. He knew all their needs because He was—and is—the great Provider.

God is the giver of every good and perfect gift—including friendship.

As Paul lay in Roman custody, he penned the phrase, "And the peace of God, which surpasses all understanding, will *guard* your hearts and your minds in Christ Jesus." Even in captivity, Paul knew that earthly security does not protect us. It is the peace of God that guards our hearts. There is no worry too big for God. Making our requests known to God is the answer for *every* situation, because God is the provider of every solution.

That includes our desire for friendship.

LET'S CHAT

Friendship started with God. People were *created* for community. God wants us to experience community with Him and with people around us. He didn't just create you for vertical friendship with Him—He made you for horizontal friendship with others. This is why friendship is something we all want desperately.

Sister, I see you. Your heart aches for friendship, and I'm right there with you.

In my current season as a new mom, friendship has changed. Some friends have distanced themselves from me because I am not as available as I used to be or because it's harder for us to relate to one another now. I feel lonely. I'm trying to find new friends while also earnestly cultivating the friendships I have left.

I see and understand your desire for real and lasting relationships. But more importantly, God sees you. Before Paul instructs us not to be anxious, he reminds

GOD IS
THE PROVIDER
OF EVERY SOLUTION.

us that the Lord is near. The Lord is in every situation, and He knows every desire of your heart. No request is too hard for Him. He is near, and He cares about your needs and desires. He is working in your situation, even if you can't feel it.

Psalm 37:4 tells us that when we delight in the Lord, He will give us the desires of our hearts. This doesn't mean God is our magic genie in a bottle, granting us the wishes we so desire. It means that the more we spend time with God, aligning our hearts with His Word, the more we will desire good things. And when we ask for good things, He gives them to us. We can have confidence that if we ask for friendship and community, God hears us and will answer. It may not happen immediately, but when we tell Him our desires, we learn to depend on Him more. He is our provider.

Don't let your desire for friendship turn into worry. Tell God what you desire. Spend daily time in His Word, delighting in who He is, and aligning your heart with His desires. Then go and be a friend. The most powerful thing you can do is be a friend. That friendship you long for? Go after it.

For a long time, I was convinced that friendship would always be scarce and anxiety-inducing. I was convinced I wouldn't have deep, meaningful relationships. But the moment I realized friendship was one of those requests that God wanted me to bring to Him, my heart changed. When we experience seasons of waiting for God to give us friends and the desire for friendship feels overwhelming and achy, we can ask Him to provide community and choose to rest in His peace that surpasses understanding.

> When we tell Him our desires, we learn to depend on Him more.

WHAT ABOUT YOU?

What anxieties and worries do you have about friendship?

What do you feel is missing in your friendships? Vulnerability? Accountability?
Write down a few things you want more of in your friendships.

Which friendships could you deepen? Invest in one of those friendships this
week.

JOURNAL YOUR PRAYERS

Thank the Lord for His peace and provision in your life. Praise Him because He loves you, He is in control, and He provides what you need.

Ask God to give you deep, meaningful, and godly friendships. Cling to the fact that the Lord is your Jehovah Jireh—your provider of every need, even friendship.

Confess your worries to God. Confess any fear that may be holding you back from pursuing friendship.

TAKE IT FURTHER TODAY

Talk to someone you wouldn't normally talk to. Reaching out to new people not only shows the love of God but also creates an opportunity to make a friend.

Write down all the people you would say are acquaintances. What relationship(s) from that list could turn into a friendship?

If you're not already plugged into a youth or young adult ministry at your local church, find one and get connected!

RESTORED

Healing from Trauma of Past Friendships

Aline T.

I was with my friends on our fourth-grade playground playing the legendary game of foursquare when someone called me an incredibly unkind name—to my face.

My jaw dropped, and my mouth grew dry. Though what she said was not true, her words weren't what hurt me.

None of my friends stood up for me or joined me as I walked away. Later that day, I got in the car and cried in my mom's arms.

When I replay the event in my mind, my body tightens, and my palms sweat. I can still feel my young heart pounding. I feel the lack of protection and care I needed from my friends.

That day wouldn't be the last time I was hurt by friends I loved. The girl who was once bold and confident became timid and unsure. I grew guarded, angry, and skeptical of people around me. That day marked the beginning of a long journey of fear and anxiety in my friendships. It created trauma I have been at war with ever since.

Read Psalm 130 and then check out the verse below.

And the God of all grace, who called you to his eternal glory in Christ, after you have suffered a little while, will himself restore you and make you strong, firm and steadfast. —1 Peter 5:10 NIV

Having had hard friendships in the past doesn't mean all our future friendships will be hard too.

For Christians, suffering is not optional. Suffering may sound like a word only severely traumatized people can use. And maybe that's you. But this big, loaded word applies to all of us because we have all experienced hardship or ongoing pain. If you are a living, breathing human, you have (or will one day) endure suffering. And that suffering may make its way into your friendships. People will fail you, and you will fail them too.

But take heart, dear friend. There is hope.

In 1 Peter, God makes a promise. Peter writes to Christians who were despised by the world. Their decision to follow Christ left them shunned by their friends and family, and they regularly faced starvation, torture, and even death. They were likely traumatized.

> Having had hard friendships in the past doesn't mean all our future friendships will be hard too.

Notice how Peter doesn't promise a life without any suffering. He doesn't even promise that a Christian's suffering will be easier than anyone else's suffering.

So, where's the hope?

God promises *He* will restore.

He will restore us.

To restore means to bring something back to its original condition. But Peter says that in addition to being restored, Christians will be made firm. God may not completely change our circumstances, but He will use all suffering to strengthen us.

LET'S CHAT

When suffering rears its head in our friendships, it can be easy to want to find a new friend. Our first inclination after being hurt often is to replace the thing that hurt us. We assume that removing the problem will fix us or heal our pain. We think a new friendship will fill the holes left by the old one. Sometimes, we become tempted to gossip about the friend who hurt us, get revenge, or even cancel her completely. We may slide into isolation, believing that the best way to protect ourselves is to not allow ourselves to be hurt again.

But the truth is, the only one capable of healing any of us is our maker. God knows you and holds the keys to true healing and freedom. If you have been hurt in a friendship and are living with the after-math of that hurt, remember what

The only one capable of healing us is our maker.

God doesn't withhold from us.

1 Peter 5:10 says: "the God of all grace ... will restore you and make you strong, firm, and steadfast" (NIV).

Every other kind of healing is cheap. Any satisfaction found outside of God is temporary. As Psalm 130 says, our healing comes as we wait on God and put all our hope in Him.

What do we do in the time between the suffering and the healing? How do we survive?

David's cry in Psalm 130 is written in that painful in-between time. He waits on the Lord, reminding himself of the truth written in God's Word. "I wait for the LORD, my whole being waits, and in his word I put my hope" (Psalm 130:5 NIV).

God doesn't withhold from us. He doesn't even need us to do anything. He offers restoration ... for *free*!

The God of all grace will *Himself* heal you. He wants to restore you. He desires to mend your heart and to make you stronger as you put your hope in Him.

I am still healing from friendship wounds. I continually ask God to replace my timidity with peace, and my guardedness with love. And when friends let me down, I need God to remind me that He will always be enough for me. When you find yourself searching for hope, remember who your healer is and put your hope in Him.

WHAT ABOUT YOU?

Have you been hurt by friends? What happened?

What do you do when friendships get hard?

Do you turn to Jesus for healing? How can you put your hope in God when you experience suffering?

JOURNAL YOUR PRAYERS.

Thank God for being your healer. Praise Him for being a God who can restore what's broken.

_____

_____

_____

_____

_____

_____

_____

_____

_____

Ask God to help you search your heart for any pain you need to give to Him. Pray that He will expose the holes within your heart, mend them, and make your spirit strong in the process.

_____

_____

_____

_____

Confess the ways you may have sought healing outside of God.

TAKE IT FURTHER TODAY.

Create a screen saver with 1 Peter 5:10 on it
to remember God's promise in suffering.

Pray for the courage to step into new friendships and then
reach out to a Christian you want to develop a friendship with.

Find an older Christian with whom you can talk about any suffering
you have experienced in your friendships. Ask her to pray with
and for you as God heals your heart.

THE GREATEST FRIEND

(Hint: It's Jesus)

Cambrie Joy

My mom always told me to be careful who I listen to. When someone's words come hurling a hundred miles an hour at me, that criticism can hurt. But I can control how deep it sinks into my heart, depending on who it's coming from.

Imagine a random stranger who spits something at you online. *Ouch.* But really? Wouldn't it hurt worse if it were someone you love? An anonymous person's words don't hold much weight because *they* don't hold much weight in your life.

So it means something dramatic when God calls us friends.

How are we going to receive that, considering who *He* is? His calling you friend holds more weight than the kindest person you know calling you friend. The Creator of the universe, who sees all our faults and sins, calls us friends even though He *knows* our brokenness. How great a friend He is! The real question is: Are we friends of God?

Read John 15:1–17 and then check out the verses below.

"Greater love has no one than this: to lay down one's life for one's friends. You are my friends if you do what I command. I no longer call you servants, because a servant does not know his master's business. Instead, I have called you friends, for everything that I learned from my Father I have made known to you."—John 15:13–15 NIV

No friend will ever love you more than Jesus.

These are Jesus's words to His disciples, and quite frankly, He couldn't have said it clearer: the disciples were His friends. But are we friends with Jesus? How did the disciples know if they were His friends? Jesus told them: ". . . if you do what I command."

Does this mean we must follow God's laws perfectly to have a friendship with Jesus? A Pharisee, one of the religious experts in Old Testament law, had the same question for Jesus. He asked, "Teacher, which is the greatest command-ment in the Law?"

No friend will ever love you more than Jesus.

Jesus replied, "'Love the Lord your God with all your heart and with all your soul and with all your mind.' This is the first and greatest commandment" (Matthew 22:36–38 NIV).

God's greatest command is that we love Him, and we love Him by accepting His Son's sacrifice for us on the cross and repenting from our old lives, which were devoid of love for God. Loving God in that way proves we are His friends.

Jesus isn't only *a* friend—He is the *greatest* friend. Jesus said there is no greater love than to lay down one's life for one's friends (John 15:13). What about laying down your life for someone who's not yet your friend? What if that someone has betrayed you? Paul, in his letter to the Romans, reminds us that this is what we did to Jesus. We were not Jesus's friends:

For one will scarcely die for a righteous person—though perhaps for a good person one would dare even to die—but God shows his love for us in that while we were still sinners, Christ died for us. (Romans 5:7–8 ESV)

There is no greater show of love than Jesus's dying for us on the cross; therefore, there is no one in the world you'd rather have calling you friend. Our sin separates us from God, and we don't deserve Jesus. He took our sin upon Himself and gave us His righteousness instead of our condemnation (2 Corinthians 5:21). What a gift! We betrayed Him, and He still laid His life down so that we could be forgiven. He calls us friends.

LET'S CHAT

You may hear a voice inside your head that says you're too far gone to be a friend of God. Don't listen to it. The Bible says Jesus died for us while we were still sinners (Romans 5:7–8). In the middle of our betrayal, wandering, denying, faith-lessness, and death in sin, Jesus chose to love us. Our sin deserved to be punished, and Jesus took that punishment for us so that we could be called friends of God. We can believe He is the greatest friend, because no greater love exists than lay-ing down your life for your friend (John 15:13).

Jesus demonstrated perfect friendship on the cross, so let's be friends of His. Let's walk with Jesus and step into a deep and rich friendship with Him, because one day, we will see His nail-scarred hands with our own eyes, and He won't shame us for putting those scars there. Instead, He'll embrace us as His *friends*.

Cultivate your friendship with Jesus. Fall in love with reading His Word, live a life of prayer that never ceases, and enjoy community with other believers who are doing the same. What a gift to be given friendship with God! Enjoy it to the fullest by giving it back to Him.

> We can believe Jesus is the greatest friend, because no greater love exists than laying down your life for your friend.

WHAT ABOUT YOU?

Do you view Jesus as your supreme friend over everyone else? How do you feel about His friendship?

How has understanding Jesus's friendship with you changed your desire to be a faithful friend to Him?

How do your friendships with other people point to your friendship with Jesus?

JOURNAL YOUR PRAYERS

Thank God for sending Jesus to give His life for you. Reflect on how great a friend Jesus is—He laid down His life for you while you were still a sinner.

_____

_____

_____

_____

_____

_____

_____

_____

_____

_____

_____

Ask God to help you see the cross clearly and to let the love of Jesus shape your heart to be more like Him, the greatest friend.

_____

_____

_____

Confess your sin to God and ask Him for forgiveness. Thank Him for choosing you to be one of Jesus's friends.

TAKE IT FURTHER TODAY

Read the book of Mark this month and note any verses about Jesus's kindness.
Notice how He interacts with His disciples and imagine Jesus having that
same kind of friendship with you.

As you go about your day and look at creation, look for Jesus in everything
around you. See how He is a friend to the birds. He takes care of them, and
that's a reminder of how He does the same for you.

Ask an older Christian how God has been a friend to him or her
over the years. As you listen, remember that God is a friend
to everyone, including you.

Compassion means entering
the suffering of another in
order to lead the way out.

—Rosaria Champagne Butterfield

WRITE YOUR STORY

Write the story of the first time you remember making a friend.

Write the story of how you met your closest friend.

Write the story of a time one of your friendships ended naturally.

Write the story of the most special thing a friend has done for you.

Write the story of the most hurtful thing a friend has done to you.

Write the story of a time you realized Jesus is your greatest friend.

Write the story of a time God ministered to you through a friend from a different generation.

Write the story of a time a friend encouraged you.

Write the story of a time a friend comforted you.

Write the story of a time a friend helped you to walk away from sin.

Write the story of a time a friend carried your burdens.

Cambria Joy

Through her YouTube channel, podcast, weekly emails, and books, Cambria Joy's passion is to help others feel healthy from the inside out. She is a certified nutrition coach, personal trainer with the National Academy of Sports Medicine, and a nutritional therapy practitioner. Cambria lives in a cozy beach town on the coast of California with her husband Bo and her tiny dog Meester.

Lauren Groves

Lauren Groves is an editor, writer, wife, mom of two, and kids' ministry coordinator in Nashville, Tennessee. She is passionate about helping kids, teens, and women know God well without needing a degree in theology or a decades-long church background. Lauren has authored *New Year, New You, Easter Changes Everything,* and a series of board books called *Toddler Theology.* Beyond writing and editing, Lauren loves family walks around her community, cooking (not baking), and cuddling under a blanket with her kids to read books.

Kolby Knell is a songwriter and speaker who lives in Nashville, Tennessee, with her husband. From an early age, Kolby found herself in the television and entertainment world, signing her first record deal at eighteen. After years of performing in churches across the country, she transitioned into speaking at young adult ministries and schools on topics like mental health, biblical femininity, and more. Kolby now writes songs and works in women's ministry at her local church. She is passionate about teaching younger generations the truth of the gospel, and that their identity can only be found in Christ.

Alexus Lee

Alexus Lee loves bringing the name of Jesus to social media. Using TikTok and other platforms, she hopes to help girls in the next generation become confident in their relationships with God and give them tools to deepen their faith and join Christian communities. Alexus is originally from a small town in Florida but now spends her days studying nursing at Liberty University, where she dreams of becoming a pediatric nurse. When she isn't studying or influencing, Alexus loves to surf, go to coffee shops, and travel anywhere adventure calls!

Gabrielle McCullough is a Minnesota-born-and-raised evangelist and Bible teacher who is eager to reach all people with the gospel of Jesus Christ. Her greatest passion is to fight for her generation to be found faithful by knowing, fearing, and loving God so that they will lead lives consecrated by holiness. Gabrielle currently resides in Waco, Texas, with her husband Cooper. She's the author of the teen girls' Bible study called *Wake Up*, which invites girls to wake up from cultural Christianity and join the mission of restoring the Word of God in the next generation. She spends the majority of her time mothering her baby boy, discipling college girls, serving at Harris Creek Baptist Church, and enjoying time with her husband Cooper!

alena T.

Alena Pitts is an actress, author, and vocalist. Alena's professional acting debut was *War Room*, a box office hit in 2015 and the sixth highest-grossing Christian film in box office history. Shortly after, Alena started on a new journey and coauthored a three-book fictional series aptly titled, Lena in the Spotlight. These books follow Alena's life in a fictional way, and they're co-authored with her mother, Wynter Pitts, author and founder of For Girls Like You Ministries. Though having experienced unbelievable success, Alena's journey has not come without loss. She tragically and unexpectedly lost her mother on July 24, 2018. Though the pain has left her and her family heartbroken, Alena is not without hope and has used her grief journey as an opportunity to share the hope found in Jesus Christ. Alena values her relationship with Jesus Christ as her highest priority, followed by her commitment to her family.

Yvonne Faith Russell

Yvonne Faith Russell is a passionate writer, editor, dancer, and choreographer. A Nashville native, she manages two careers in publishing and the performing arts. She is the author of *A Word to the Wise: Lessons I Learned at 22* and *Mature & Complete: A Devotional Journal for Healing, Value, and Satisfaction in Christ*. In addition to publishing, Yvonne Faith works as a professional dance artist in Washington, DC, and has performed at many venues across the United States, including the John F. Kennedy Center for the Performing Arts. To learn more about Yvonne Faith, visit her website at www.yvonnefaithrussell.com.

Tara Sun

Tara Sun is the author of *Surrender Your Story*, host of the popular podcast, *Truth Talks with Tara*, and proud wife and boy mom. She is passionate about helping women simplify what it means to live out the gospel and know, love, and live God's Word through online resources. Tara lives in Oregon with her husband, Michael, and their son, Hunter. When she isn't writing or podcasting, Tara loves to cook, bake sourdough, go on walks through their small town, and chat about Jesus and life with anyone and everyone.

Tega Faafa Taylor is the brand owner and content editor for Hyfi Students. She lives in metro Atlanta, Georgia, with her husband and is a graduate from Dallas Theological Seminary. She also has a neuroscience degree and has worked with various churches, camps, and conferences as a teacher, speaker, spoken word artist, and host. Tega loves sharing how God is relevant in today's culture and how Jesus changes every part of our lives. Outside of ministry, Tega loves thrifting, fashion, podcasting, music, pop culture, TikTok, and reading on her Kindle.

Works Cited

Lewis, C. S., W. H. Lewis, and Walter Hooper. *Letters of C. S. Lewis*. San Francisco: HarperOne, 2017.

Lash, Joseph P. *Helen and Teacher: The Story of Helen Keller and Anne Sullivan Macy*. Cambridge, MA: Perseus Publishing, 1997.

Carmichael, Amy. "Review of I Know Nothing of Calvary Love." SermonIndex. net. Accessed December 19, 2023. https://www.sermonindex.net/modules/ articles/index.php?view=article&aid=20754.

Gallagher, Conor. *If Aristotle's Kid Had an iPod: Ancient Wisdom for Modern Parents*. Charlotte, NC: Saint Benedict Press, 2014.

Keller, Timothy. *The Meaning of Marriage: Facing the Complexities of Commitment with the Wisdom of God*. New York, NY: Penguin, 2013.

Bonhoeffer, Dietrich. *Life Together: A Classic Exploration of Christian Community*. San Francisco, CA: HarperOne, 1978.

Peterson, Andrew. *Adorning the Dark: Thoughts on Community, Calling, and the Mystery of Making*. Nashville, TN: B&H Publishing, 2019.

Hill Perry, Jackie. "Love Is a Gospel Issue." *The Gospel Coalition,* 2018.

Butterfield, Rosaria Champagne. *The Secret Thoughts of an Unlikely Convert: An English Professor's Journey into Christian Faith*. Pittsburgh, PA: Crown & Covenant Publications, 2012.

WHAT A FRIEND WE HAVE IN JESUS

What a Friend we have in Jesus,
All our sins and griefs to bear!
What a privilege to carry
Everything to God in prayer!
O what peace we often forfeit,
O what needless pain we bear,
All because we do not carry
Everything to God in prayer!

Have we trials and temptations?
Is there trouble anywhere?
We should never be discouraged,
Take it to the Lord in prayer.
Can we find a friend so faithful
Who will all our sorrows share?
Jesus knows our every weakness,
Take it to the Lord in prayer.

Are we weak and heavy-laden,
Cumbered with a load of care?
Precious Savior, still our refuge—
Take it to the Lord in prayer;
Do thy friends despise, forsake thee?
Take it to the Lord in prayer;
In His arms He'll take and shield thee,
Thou wilt find a solace there.